Mobile Learning

for AI

I dedicate this book to the person who, for the last twelve years, has been the inspiration for everything I have done in my life: my daughter Katherine.

Mobile Learning
for ALL

Supporting Accessibility With the iPad

Luis Pérez

CORWIN
A SAGE Company

CORWIN
A SAGE Company

FOR INFORMATION:

Corwin
A SAGE Company
2455 Teller Road
Thousand Oaks, California 91320
(800) 233-9936
www.corwin.com

SAGE Publications Ltd.
1 Oliver's Yard
55 City Road
London, EC1Y 1SP
United Kingdom

SAGE Publications India Pvt. Ltd.
B 1/I 1 Mohan Cooperative Industrial Area
Mathura Road, New Delhi 110 044
India

SAGE Publications Asia-Pacific Pte. Ltd.
3 Church Street
#10–04 Samsung Hub
Singapore 049483

Acquisitions Editor: Arnis Burvikovs
Associate Editor: Desirée A. Bartlett
Editorial Assistant: Mayan White
Permissions Editor: Jennifer Barron
Project Editor: Veronica Stapleton
Copy Editor: Codi Bowman
Typesetter: Hurix Systems Private Ltd.
Proofreader: Dennis W. Webb
Indexer: Jean Casalegno
Cover Designer: Anupama Krishnan

The screenshots in this book are from Apple (http://www.apple.com/legal/contact/), Nuance (http://www.nuance.com/company/company-overview/company-policies/legal-notices/index.htm), and Behavior Tracker Pro (https://www.behaviortrackerpro.com/).

Printed in the United States of America

Library of Congress Cataloging-in-Publication Data

Pérez, Luis Felipe.
Mobile learning for all : supporting accessibility with the iPad / Luis Perez.

pages cm

Includes bibliographical references and index.

ISBN 978-1-4522-5855-3 (pbk.)

1. Computer-assisted instruction. 2. iPad (Computer) I. Title.

LB1028.5.P425 2013

371.33'4—dc23

2013005346

This book is printed on acid-free paper.

13 14 15 16 17 10 9 8 7 6 5 4 3 2 1

Contents

List of Figures

List of Codes

Preface

Mobile Learning for All provides practical information for teachers and other educational professionals who want to learn how to use the iPad to meet the needs of all learners. Each chapter not only includes a discussion of the accessibility features built into the iPad and related apps, but also how these features support one or more guidelines of Universal Design for Learning (UDL). UDL is a framework for designing flexible learning environments that take into account the diversity of the student population by building in features that allow a broad set of learners to access learning. UDL is based on the idea that all learners differ in the ways in which they perceive and comprehend the information presented to them, and it seeks to eliminate barriers to learning that can prevent some students from accomplishing their learning goals. For example, a student with a visual disability may require information to be presented in a different format from other learners (such as audio or braille), while a struggling reader may comprehend the information faster or more efficiently when it's presented through multiple modalities (text and audio) rather than through printed text alone. The idea that learning should be flexible and accommodate the needs of a variety of learners is a central tenet of UDL.

Intended Audience

While many of the iPad accessibility features discussed in this book were developed for people with disabilities, with some creativity many of them can be used to accommodate the needs of other diverse learners (such as English language learners and struggling readers) in the general education classroom. Thus, while the primary audience includes teachers, parents, and related service providers (occupational, speech, and physical therapists) who work with students with disabilities at all levels (K–20), the information in the book could prove helpful to general education teachers as well. The book could also be used in teacher preparation programs to ensure that preservice teachers learn about the range of accessibility features they can use with their students once they enter the teaching profession.

Special Features

To give the readers an opportunity to practice what they have learned, each chapter includes a series of activities designed to make educators more familiar with the accessibility features of their iPads. For example, in the chapter that focuses on learning and literacy, I have the reader enable the Speak Selection (text to speech) feature, then practice selecting text in a book in the iBooks app and listening to it read aloud by the built-in voice. Each chapter also includes a section dedicated to apps that complement the accessibility features discussed in that chapter. The word app is shorthand for application, and the term refers to the small, specialized programs that can be downloaded and installed on the iPad. These apps, which can be purchased or downloaded from Apple's App Store, often include additional features that extend what can be done with the iPad. For each app mentioned in the book, I have provided its price at the time of writing, but readers should understand that apps frequently go on sale or add features that lead developers to charge more for them.

This book also represents an attempt to address the need for information about accessibility and mobile learning with a unique approach. In addition to the text, the book includes a series of QR codes. A QR code is a special type of barcode that is often used in print to provide a link to an online resource such as a web page or video. When the code is scanned with QR code reader app, the web page or video will open on the mobile device with the appropriate app for accessing that type of content (such as the Safari web browser for web pages or the YouTube app for videos hosted on that service). Using a free QR code reader app (such as the free QR Reader for iPhone, which also runs on the iPad), scan QR code P.1 to learn more about this technology (or go to http://en.wikipedia.org/wiki/QR_code).

QR Code P.1 Entry for QR Code on Wikipedia.

Each QR code in the book can be scanned to open video tutorials and other online resources that can be updated as new accessibility features for the iPad are released or updated. I have also created a blog to provide updates on any developments related to iPad accessibility (such as new product announcements from Apple, feature upgrades, new apps, etc.). The blog is available at http://mobile-learning4allbook.wordpress.com, and you can subscribe to receive updates as they become available. Along with the blog, I have created a Pinterest site where I have organized the many apps mentioned in the book into categories that are easy to browse and provide direct links for downloading the apps from the App Store. This Pinterest site is available at http://pinterest.com/mlearning4all/.

Through the blog, tutorial videos, and other online resources, the book is meant to be a living, dynamic resource that will keep up with the fast development of technology. The inclusion of links (in the form of QR codes) to videos and other resources is also in keeping with my commitment to present information in a way that meets the needs of students with diverse learning styles as well. Thus, each of the video tutorials includes closed captioning to ensure its accessibility to viewers who have hearing disabilities as well as to facilitate its use in different environments (such as in a noisy classroom or teachers' lounge). My experience as a web accessibility professional has allowed me to create the video tutorials in a way that itself contributes to the overall accessibility of this project.

With *Mobile Learning for All,* you have everything you need to get started with building a toolkit for implementing UDL with the iPad in your classroom, including the following.

- In-depth coverage of all of the built-in accessibility features of the iPad, including the latest features introduced with the iOS 6 update
- Access to more than 20 closed captioned video tutorials with step-by-step directions you can review at any time, including from your iPad
- Discussion of more than 150 apps that have been carefully curated by the author based on his experiences working with people with disabilities across a range of different settings (K–12 schools, higher education, research, and professional practice as an Apple Distinguished Educator)

Acknowledgments

No person is an island. I consider myself lucky to have met many exceptional people over the years that have been willing to generously share their knowledge and expertise with me.

I especially wish to thank the Apple Distinguished Educator community. I am humbled to be part of such a talented, knowledgeable, and passionate group of educators. In particular, I wish to acknowledge the support I have received from the members of our Inclusive Design Group: Greg Alchin, Phyllis Brodsky, Mark Coppin, Mark Dohn, Sarah Herrlinger, Madaleine Pagliese, Cherie Pickering, and Megan Wilson. I hope you find this book a valuable contribution toward the work we do to provide a more inclusive educational experience for all students.

To the team at the Florida Center for Instructional Technology, I appreciate your support of my work over the years, and I thank you for giving me the opportunity to grow in my knowledge of accessibility as I developed the content for the Tech Ease websites.

A sincere thank you to all of my friends who have been there to provide support in both small and big ways over the many years I have been in school: Heather, BJ, Cara and Rob, Euna, Kris and Gillian, Shannon, and anyone I have forgotten to mention. I appreciate your friendship more than you know.

Cindy, for making my life better in so many ways, thank you. And the biggest thanks of all to my mom, Lidia. Without the many sacrifices you made to bring me to this wonderful country, none of what I have been able to accomplish in my life would have been possible. I also want to acknowledge my dad, Luis Felipe. Although I have not seen you as much as I would have liked over the course of my life, you and my entire family in the Dominican Republic have always been close to my heart. The books you bought me as a child inspired a passion for learning that continues to this day.

Finally, I want to thank two special gentlemen who were role models and influenced the course of my life in a significant way: our family friend Julio, who took my brother and me under his wing at a vulnerable time in our lives and showed us how we could be strong, successful Dominican men, and Rick Newton, my advisor at the Westtown School who pushed me to have high expectations for myself and modeled a life of learning dedicated to social justice and the common good.

At Corwin, I wish to thank Debra Stollenwerk, Desirée Bartlett, Kim Greenberg, Veronica Hooper, Mayan White, and Codi Bowman for making the process of getting this book published such a valuable learning experience for me.

Publisher's Acknowledgments

Corwin wishes to acknowledge the following peer reviewers for their editorial insight and guidance.

Dr. Debi Gartland, Professor of Special Education
Towson University
Department of Special Education
Towson, MD

Dr. Carol S. Holzberg, Technology Coordinator
Greenfield Public Schools
Greenfield, MA

Cheryl S. Oakes, Resource Room Teacher
Wells High School
Wells, ME

Dr. J. David Smith, Professor Emeritus
University of North Carolina at Greensboro

About the Author

Luis Pérez, Phd earned his doctorate in special education from the University of South Florida. His research interests include technology professional development for teachers, assistive technology, universal design, web accessibility, and disability studies. He also received his M. Ed. in instructional technology from the University of South Florida, where he is on the staff of the Florida Center for Instructional Technology. At FCIT, Luis developed Tech Ease 4 All, a collection of assistive technology tutorials for parents, teachers, and other professionals who work with students who have special needs.

Luis was selected to be an Apple Distinguished Educator in 2009, and he is a frequent presenter at regional, national, and international conferences on educational technology and accessibility, including the Florida Educational Technology Conference (FETC), the International Society for Technology in Education (ISTE) conference, Closing the Gap, and the International Technology and Persons with Disabilities Conference (CSUN).

Luis was diagnosed with retinitis pigmentosa, an eye condition that results in progressive vision loss, at the age of 29. Luis is considered legally blind due to the fact that he only has about 10 degrees of central vision left. As a person with a visual disability, Luis knows firsthand what a difference mobile technology can make in the lives of people with disabilities. Despite his limited eyesight, Luis is an avid photographer who relies on his iPhone and iPad as his primary means of capturing and editing images.

Introduction

The first Apple mobile device to include accessibility features was the third generation iPod shuffle, which Apple announced as the "first music player that talks to you" when it was released in early 2009. A few months later, Apple followed up with the release of the iPhone 3GS and the third generation iPod touch, two new touch screen devices that also had the VoiceOver screen reader already available on the Mac. While some educators used these devices in their classrooms, the adoption of Apple mobile devices in education really kicked into high gear with the release of the iPad in 2010. Since then, a number of schools and universities across the nation have started programs to provide iPads for their students, and parents and students have acquired them for personal use even where no iPad program exists in their schools. According to Phil Schiller, Apple's head of marketing, there were about 1.5 million iPads in use in educational settings as of January 2012 (Apple, 2012).

The rapid adoption of the iPad in the education space has occurred despite the fact that research on how the use of these mobile devices impacts student outcomes is just starting to emerge. A recent study by textbook publisher Houghton Mifflin found that students using an Algebra 1 text on the iPad scored "proficient" or "advanced" in subject comprehension at a higher rate (78% compared to 59%) than students using the paper textbook counterpart (Bonnington, 2012). Similarly, a study by Motion Math Games found that fifth graders who played the game Motion Math for 20 minutes a day over a five-day period saw an increase in their test scores of 15% on average (Riconscente, 2011). It remains to be seen if independently conducted research (not sponsored by Apple, the textbook publishers, or app developers) will yield similar empirical evidence on the impact of the iPad on student outcomes. However, blogs and other online discussions involving parents, teachers, and other educational professionals continue to provide anecdotal evidence of the device's impact in the lives of students.

One segment of the education space that has been especially receptive to the iPad is that of special education, where the devices have been welcomed into the classroom by both teachers and other professionals such as speech language pathologists and assistive technology specialists. A number of factors make the iPad especially helpful for students who have special needs:

- The device has a larger screen than other mobile devices, providing sufficient space to display the symbols used in many communication systems for students who have speech difficulties.
- Solutions based around the iPad sometimes cost much less than those based on specialized devices. For example, the stand-alone communication devices used by many people with speech difficulties can sometimes cost around $8,000. An iPad loaded with several communication apps that perform the same functions can be obtained for under $1,000, a significant cost savings for students with disabilities and their families.
- At 1.44 pounds for the latest version, the device is lightweight enough for even young children and some students with motor disabilities to handle and operate on their own.
- The iPad's long battery life (about 10 hours according to Apple) makes it ideal for students who must rely on their device for communication and other needs over the course of a typical school day.
- The device can be customized to meet the needs of individual students through the more than 200,000 iPad apps currently available on the App Store.
- The device enjoys a high degree of social acceptability that appeals to students and parents wanting to avoid the stigma often associated with disabilities. As one parent stated, "The iPad is also used by typical children, so it makes our kids part of the 'in' crowd" (Boyd, 2011).
- Apple has included a number of built-in accessibility features to enable people with disabilities to use their devices, including a screen reader for people with visual disabilities, an AssistiveTouch feature for those who have motor difficulties, and support for captions as well as alternatives to audible alerts for those who have hearing loss.

This last point is important in light of U.S. laws that require educational technologies to be accessible to students with disabilities. The iPad is well positioned in this regard because Apple has a long history of incorporating accessibility into the design of its products, and currently, almost every mobile device it makes (the one exception is the iPod classic) includes accessibility features out of the box. Other companies have taken notice of Apple's success with the iPad, and many competing tablets are now starting to incorporate similar accessibility features.

Unfortunately, many educators not only are unaware of their legal responsibilities to provide accessibility, but they may also not know that many of the technologies that will help them meet the requirements of the law are already available for free or at a very low cost. This book aims to make teachers and other educational professionals more aware of the many accessibility features that are available on the iPad to accommodate the needs of diverse learners, including students with disabilities. Through the step-by-step tutorials and practice activities included in this book, these educational professionals will become more proficient in the use of these accessibility features. One could argue that we are living through the second wave of accessibility. Most of the technologies needed by people with disabilities (screen readers, hearing aids, switch access, etc.) have been invented or are in the last stages of development. Thus, knowledge about the appropriate use of technology, not its availability, has often been the barrier that prevents it from transforming instructional practices in favor of inclusion and equal participation by all. In the second wave of accessibility, the challenge will be to educate teachers and other educational professionals about the many available tools and strategies they could be using to provide accessibility for all their students.

In addition to the built-in accessibility features that make the iPad accessible to students with a range of special needs, educators also can select from among the more than 200,000 educational apps currently on the market. The marketing slogan, "There's an app for that," captures the flexibility the iPad and other Apple mobile devices provide to educators for meeting the needs of a diverse student population. In this book, educators will also learn about a number of apps for students with various sensory and motor disabilities, as well as apps for meeting basic needs for communication, organization, and other life skills that promote independence and quality of life for students with special needs. Along with those apps that facilitate daily living for people with disabilities in general, it is also important to highlight apps that support the development of literacy, numeracy, and other academic skills. These apps can provide the supports many students with special needs need to access the general education curriculum. The support for third-party apps on Apple's mobile devices also opens a world of possibility by allowing anyone to develop an app if there is a need that is not met by a built-in feature or an existing app. Not surprisingly, a few apps have been developed by parents looking for solutions that would allow their children who have special needs to have access to the same opportunities as other learners.

The goal of providing access to learning for all students is one of the cornerstones of Universal Design for Learning (UDL), a concept explored in more detail in later chapters. The focus here has been the "why" of universal design and accessibility (the rationale for teaching with these concepts in mind) while the rest of the book will focus on the "how" (making accessibility and universal design a reality by selecting and implementing the appropriate tools for specific student needs).

1

Universal Design and Mobile Learning

Defining Universal Design

The term *universal design* (UD) traces its origin to the field of architecture. Ronald L. Mace, who is credited with coining the term, defined it as the design of all products and the built environment to be aesthetic and usable to the greatest extent possible by everyone, regardless of their age, ability, or status in life (Center for Universal Design, 2010). A good example of universal design is the addition of ramps to buildings to allow people in wheelchairs to access them independently. While these ramps were intended for people with disabilities, they can also benefit other groups, such as mothers with children in strollers and delivery staff. The Center for Universal Design (2010) has developed a set of seven principles for the universal design of products and environments, and I encourage you to visit their website (http://www.ncsu.edu/project/design-projects/udi/) for more information about these design principles: (1) equitable use, (2) flexibility in use, (3) simple and intuitive use, (4) perceptible information, (5) tolerance for error, (6) low physical effort, and (7) size and space for approach and use.

The iPad meets many of the requirements for universally designed products. Many of the qualities that make this device attractive to the general public (its portability, for example) also makes it well suited to meet the need many people with disabilities have for a small and lightweight device that is always with them to meet communication and other access needs (UD principle: low physical effort). The touch screen interface of the iPad is also intuitive and can be easily learned by even young children as seen on a YouTube video at http://bit.ly/iPadfirstencounter (UD principle: simple and intuitive use). The iPad is also highly customizable through its support for a variety of apps (UD principle: flexibility in use) as well as its built-in features for making information easier to perceive for people with vision or hearing loss (UD principle: perceptible information). One of the appeals of the iPad for working with individuals with disabilities is that as a consumer device marketed to the general public it does not have the same stigma attached to it as more specialized devices that are closely identified with one particular group of users (UD principle: equitable use).

Defining Universal Design for Learning (UDL)

While it originated in the discipline of architecture, the principles of universal design have been applied in other fields. For example, the Center for Applied Special Technology (CAST) has developed a framework for the design of learning environments that is based on universal design principles. This framework is called *Universal Design for Learning* (UDL), and it provides a blueprint for creating instructional goals, methods, materials, and assessments that work for everyone (CAST, n.d.).

Rather than recommending a one-size-fits-all solution, UDL calls for flexible approaches that can be customized and adjusted for individual learning needs (CAST, n.d.). The UDL framework seeks to meet the needs of diverse learners by engaging the three brain networks researchers have identified (CAST):

- The recognition network (the "what" of learning) is engaged when students gather facts and categorize what they see, hear, and read.
- The strategic network (the "how" of learning) is engaged when students organize and express their ideas. Examples of the strategic network in action include writing an essay or solving a math problem.

- The engagement network (the "why" of learning) refers to affective dimensions of learning, such as how learners are motivated, challenged, and kept interested in the learning task.

The way in which these three networks are engaged is different from one learner to the next. To account for these differences, UDL provides for variety and flexibility along three dimensions addressed through the following design principles (CAST, 2011):

- *Multiple and flexible means of representation:* the teacher presents information in different ways to accommodate the needs of those with sensory disabilities (vision or hearing loss), learning disabilities, language or cultural differences, and different learning styles (auditory or visual).
- *Multiple and flexible means of action and expression:* the teacher provides options for learners to navigate the learning environment and express what they know in different ways. For example, the teacher may allow a student who has difficulty organizing his or her thoughts on paper to present the same information in a movie or a slideshow.
- *Multiple and flexible means of engagement:* learning is made relevant by appealing to the learner's personal interests and life experiences and by providing multiple options for what is learned and how learning takes place (individually or in groups). Learners are also taught coping skills that will promote the development of self-regulation.

A key goal of UDL is the personalization of learning so that it is not a one-size-fits-all approach but instead responds to the individual needs of each learner. Another goal of UDL is the elimination of barriers that can keep certain students, such as students with disabilities, from having access to the curriculum. To help teachers move toward this goal, each UDL principle is further broken down into a set of guidelines that provide practical advice for implementing UDL in the classroom. Throughout this book, I will focus on the ways in which the built-in accessibility features of the iPad can be used to support the implementation of UDL guidelines in our schools to create learning environments that allow all learners, including those who have disabilities, to be successful.

As I introduce each of the accessibility features of the iPad and the apps available for this device, I will attempt to map them to one or more of the UDL guidelines. However, these suggestions are only meant as a starting point for implementing UDL with these mobile devices. You may be able to come up with additional applications I have overlooked, and that's perfectly fine. I encourage you to experiment and find even more creative and innovative ways to use the iPad to meet the specific needs of people with disabilities in your setting.

Benefits of Universal Design

The premise at the heart of universal design is that it benefits everyone. However, universal design also levels the playing field for some individuals who may be excluded from equal participation when universal design is not considered. The following scenarios demonstrate the wide range of people who can benefit from the accessibility and universal design features built into the iPad:

- Debbie is a six-year-old student who was diagnosed with autism spectrum disorder. Because of her communication challenges, she often has difficulty expressing her basic needs. Using an app called Proloqu02Go, Debbie can express her basic needs and also continue to build her vocabulary for later in life.
- David is an eighth-grade student whose dyslexia makes it difficult for him to read the books assigned for homework. Fortunately, David's teacher attended a presentation where she learned about several text-to-speech apps David can use to have his iPad read aloud to him. One of those apps has a highlighting feature that allows David to see what the words look like and hear what they sound like at the same time. The combination has been effective in helping David improve his reading.
- Steve is a high school student who has been blind since birth. He uses the iBooks app on his iPad with VoiceOver to read the latest New York Times best sellers and participate in an after-school book club with other students with disabilities. The book club has been a big source of support and social interaction for Steve.
- Tom is a college student who was recently diagnosed with attention deficit disorder. One of Tom's challenges is staying organized and ensuring he can meet the deadlines for the four courses he takes each semester. Tom uses several apps on his iPad to keep track of assignment deadlines. He also uses Pages, the iPad version of Apple's word processing program, to take notes during class.

These are just a few examples of the wide range of applications for Apple mobile devices for students with disabilities at all levels of education. With support for third-party apps, the potential of the devices for students with disabilities is only limited by the imagination of parents, teachers, and developers.

Accessibility, Ethics, and the Law

Aside from improved usability and better user experience provided by universal design, accessibility is a legal requirement. Section 504 of the Rehabilitation Act of 1973, prohibits discrimination against people with disabilities in any program that receives federal funding, including K–12 schools and institutions of higher learning. Under the Individuals with Disabilities Education Act (IDEA), school districts are required to provide assistive technology when it supports the student's acquisition of a free and appropriate public education. In determining a student's needs, as part of the IEP process, IDEA requires that assistive technology be considered. Furthermore, the 2004 reauthorization of IDEA added requirements pertaining to the timely provision of accessible instructional materials (AIM) to students with print disabilities. The rights of students with disabilities are also protected under Title II of the Americans with Disabilities Act (ADA) of 1990, which applies to all entities of state and local government, including public schools, colleges, and universities.

In response to the increasing use of e-readers and other emerging technologies in education, the U.S. Department of Education recently issued a Dear Colleague Letter (DCL) to college and university presidents (U. S. Department of Education, 2010). The purpose of the DCL was to clarify how the ADA and Section 504 apply to emerging technology such as e-readers. According to the DCL, the application of the nondiscrimination requirements of Section 504 and the ADA means that schools must ensure that emerging technology, such as e-readers, is fully accessible to students who are blind or have low vision. However, it is not just students with visual disabilities who are protected under these laws. In the DCL, the Department of Education added that students with specific learning disabilities that make it difficult for them to get information from printed sources (those students who have "print disabilities") are also protected under U.S. disability laws. While the DCL was addressed to college and university presidents, it contained a section that clearly stated that elementary and secondary schools have the same legal obligations toward students with disabilities.

While meeting legal requirements may be a good reason for implementing only those technologies that have accessibility support in schools, a more important consideration is the ethical responsibility educators have to their students. We currently live in an age of rapid change in which full participation in the digital economy depends on access to information and knowledge. As educators, we have a responsibility to provide students with the tools and skills they will need to have access to the same opportunities as other members of society. By selecting technologies that implement universal design and accessibility, we will not only be ensuring students can participate in the classroom today, we will be preparing them with the skills they will need to function as productive, independent members of society in the future.

I hope that after reading this chapter you have a better understanding of the legal and ethical responsibilities we have as educators when it comes to accessibility. With its many built-in accessibility features, the iPad incorporates many of the universal design principles discussed in this chapter. Along with the wide selection of apps in the App Store, the iPad also provides educators with the flexibility required for implementing universal design for learning to meet the needs of a diverse student population. In the next chapter, I provide an overview of the many peripherals and accessories you can purchase to further adapt the iPad to meet specific student needs. I also introduce the accessibility features that will be discussed in more detail in the remaining chapters of the books. The reader will learn where to go to enable or disable these accessibility features, as well as how to update an iPad to the latest version of iOS to take advantage of new features as they are made available.

2

Getting Started
With Accessibility
on the iPad

his chapter will provide an overview of the many peripherals and
accessories you can add to your toolkit for using the iPad with
students who have special needs. You will also learn how to enable
the accessibility features that will be discussed in more detail in the
remaining chapters of the book and how to update your devices
when Apple releases new accessibility features and improvements.

The iPad

When Apple released the original version of the iPad in April 2010,
it quickly became a big hit in education, especially with families and
educators who support students with special needs. Its larger screen
compared to other mobile devices makes the iPad easier to use for
students with limited motor skills who might find it difficult to tap
icons on a smaller screen. In addition to a larger screen, the iPad features a long-lasting battery, which allows for extended periods of use
without requiring a charge. This is important for applications that
must be available over long periods, such as communication apps
that provide students with a voice to allow them to express their basic
needs to others.

Since the device has only been on the market a few years, you may still find any of the following versions of the iPad in use:

- iPad (first generation): The original version of the iPad did not have any cameras, and it is no longer supported in iOS 6. The only way to import photos into apps with this device is through a special camera connector kit from Apple (available for $29). The kit includes two options for importing photos: using the camera's USB cable or directly from an SD memory card.
- iPad 2: The second generation of the device was the first to feature front and back cameras. The front camera was designed to support the FaceTime video chat app. The device was much thinner and lighter than the original version, and it featured a processor that Apple claimed was twice as fast as the original iPad. At the time of writing, Apple is still selling this model in its online store, but only in two 16GB models (one of which supports 3G cellular connectivity). Many schools have opted to purchase the iPad 2 because of its lower price of $399 for the Wi-Fi-only version at the time of writing.
- New iPad (third generation): This short-lived model was introduced in March of 2012, and quickly discontinued in October of the same year. It was the first version of the iPad with a high-resolution Retina display and support for 4G LTE cellular connectivity. The new iPad also saw a significant upgrade to the quality of its cameras, with the back camera capable of capturing 5MP photos as compared to less than 1MP in the previous version.
- iPad with Retina display (fourth generation): The most recent version of the iPad at the time of writing is equipped with a faster processor that Apple claims is twice as fast as the one in the previous version. This is the first model of the iPad to feature a new Lightning connector Apple has designed to replace the older 40-pin connector used by previous models. This change will require owners of this iPad version to upgrade any peripherals that use the 40-pin connector if they want to continue to use them with their iPads. The fourth generation iPad is available in 16GB, 32GB, 64 GB, and 128 GB and starts at $499.
- iPad mini: A smaller, 7.9 inch version of the iPad was released alongside the fourth generation 9.7-inch iPad in October 2012. The iPad mini is similar to the iPad 2 in terms of its components. It has the same processor and display, but it uses the Lightning connector instead of the 40-pin one. The iPad mini is

available in the same configurations as the fourth-generation iPad (16GB, 32GB, and 64GB with options for Wi-Fi only or 4G cellular connectivity), and it starts at $329.

While all versions of the iPad starting with the iPad 2 can run iOS 6, not all features are supported across the different models. For example, the dictation feature and the Siri personal assistant are only supported with the new iPad (third generation) or later. One thing to consider as you look at the choices of iPad models is that as apps are updated to support the new Retina displays their size will increase dramatically, and your iPad will be able to hold fewer apps and content than before. For this reason, I recommend educators opt for the 32GB model that can be purchased with twice the storage as the base model for only $100 or so more. Many apps for students with special needs also include high-quality voices and many symbol libraries that take up space along with the other graphics needed by the app.

Accessories

The functionality of your iPad can be enhanced by a few accessories if you or someone you work with has special needs. These accessories range from consumer products that are not specifically designed for people with disabilities (such as the Apple Wireless Keyboard) to new switch access technologies designed for people with motor and cognitive disabilities. A wide selection of cases and stands is also available to protect the devices from drops and other damage. If you work with students who have behavior or emotional challenges, I cannot stress enough the importance of making sure your devices are protected by a sturdy case. I found this out the hard way when one of the preservice teachers I work with had her iPad thrown across the room by the student she was working with, cracking the screen and rendering the device unusable.

Cases, Stands, and Mounts

While the iPad is built to withstand quite a bit of abuse, it would be a good idea to protect the device with a sturdy case if you plan to use it with someone who might not be able to hold it firmly. Several companies make rugged cases for the iPad, including Gripcase, M–Edge, Griffin, Incipio, Trident (Kraken series for iPad), AMDi (the iAdapter case includes integrated speakers for AAC users), and Gumdrop. The Aquapac cases are a good option if you need to protect the devices from any kind of liquid. RJ Cooper makes a Bumper Case that can be combined with a Carrying Case for on-the-go protection of the iPad. The Carrying Case includes a shoulder strap to make it easier to carry the iPad while active.

RJ Cooper sells two stands for the iPad: a fixed angle stand with a special Stick & Suck solution to keep the stand from skidding, and a variable-angle stand that also includes nonskid feet. The variable-angle stand collapses flat for travel. The Stabile stand from Thought Out (www.thoughtout.biz) is another sturdy stand made from solid steel that will hold an iPad at a 55-degree angle in either landscape or portrait mode. The suction mounts from AbleNet provide a way to secure the iPad to any flat surface using a twist-lock suction base.

For people who use a wheelchair, a number of companies make mounting systems for iOS devices. RJ Cooper makes a number of mounts ranging in price from $119 to $149. These mounts can be purchased on the RJ Cooper website at www.rjcooper.com. Beyond Adaptive (www.beyondadaptive.com) also makes several wheelchair mounting kits, including some with a quick release mount for an iPad. Many of the AbleNet mounting solutions can be used to support an iPad when paired with a mounting plate or cradle (available for purchase on the AbleNet website at www.ablenetinc.com).

Wireless Keyboards

Some people with visual impairments may find it easier to input text with a physical keyboard rather than using the onscreen keyboard on their iPad. The Apple wireless keyboard ($69) is a Bluetooth keyboard compatible with an iPad running iOS 4.0 or later. To use the Apple wireless keyboard with your iPad, you must first pair the two (see Figures 2.1 and 2.2).

1. Open the Settings app and choose Bluetooth on the left side of the screen.

Figure 2.1   Bluetooth Option in Settings

2. Turn Bluetooth on by tapping the On/Off switch.

Figure 2.2　On/Off Switch for Bluetooth in Settings

3. Turn the keyboard on (the power button is found on the right side, just above the eject key
4. Once the keyboard is recognized, tap its name under Devices. You should then see a prompt with a passkey you will need to enter on the keyboard to finish pairing it with your iPad.

Figure 2.3　Prompt for Pairing a Bluetooth Keyboard on the iPad

Once paired, the external keyboard will be used in place of the onscreen keyboard for entering text, but you can still use the onscreen keyboard by pressing the Eject key on the external keyboard. When using the external keyboard, some basic keyboard shortcuts will be available:

- Command + A: select all
- Command + X: cut the selected text
- Command + C: copy the selected text
- Command + V: paste the selected text
- Command + Z: undo the last action

The keyboard's volume, screen brightness, and playback controls will also work as expected. A number of cases with built-in keyboards are available from companies such as Belkin, Zagg, Kensington, and Logitech. The Bluetooth keyboards on these cases work much like Apple's wireless keyboard, and the pairing process is the same as with that keyboard.

Braille Displays

The iPad has support for more than 40 different refreshable braille displays. A full list of compatible devices can be found on the Apple Accessibility site at www.apple.com/accessibility/iphone/braille-display.html.

Instead of using synthesized speech, a refreshable braille display outputs the information that would normally be read aloud by VoiceOver as braille on a separate device connected with Bluetooth. The steps for setting up a refreshable braille display to work with your iOS device are very similar to those for setting a wireless keyboard:

1. Go to Settings > Bluetooth.
2. Turn Bluetooth on by tapping the On/Off switch.
3. Go to Settings > General > Accessibility > VoiceOver > Braille.
4. Choose the braille display by tapping its name.

One thing to note about using a braille display with an iPad is that the Bluetooth connection can use your battery faster when it is turned on. If you plan to use Bluetooth a lot (with or without a braille display), you may want to purchase an additional battery pack for your device. Several companies make such battery packs, including some that are built into a case for your iPad. The one that I use with my iPad is made by Mophie (www.mophie.com). I opted for an external unit (instead of one built into a case) as it gives me the flexibility to connect it to any of my devices, not just the one that fits into a specific case.

Earphones and Hearing Aid Accessories

The Apple Earpods include a microphone that doubles as a button for answering phone calls and controlling music playback. These earphones are available for $29 at any Apple retail store or online through the Apple Store. Depending on the number of times you press the center button on the earphones' microphone, you can activate different features on your iPad:

- Press the button once to start or stop music playback.
- While listening to music or an audiobook, press the button twice to fast-forward to the next song, and press it three times to move to the previous song.
- Press and hold the button for a few seconds to activate Siri, the personal assistant feature available on the third generation iPad. Press it one more time to dismiss Siri.
- In compatible photography apps (such as the built-in Camera app or Camera +), press the volume up button once to take a picture.

In addition to Apple, a number of companies now make headphones with microphones that are compatible with the iOS devices, such as the iPhone. People with hearing impairments can use a T-coil inductive ear loop such as TecEar's T-Link (which also has a microphone) or Music Link for better audio through their T-coil enabled hearing aid or cochlear implant. The T-Link and Music Link can be purchased on the TecEar website at www.tecear.com/TLink.htm. "Made for iPhone" Bluetooth hearing aids that promise to deliver a better audio experience while providing better power consumption are also supported by iOS 6.

Switch Interfaces

At its most basic, a switch is a device (usually a button) that a person with a motor or cognitive disability can press to make a selection. Some switch systems support scanning, where the switch is paired with appropriate software that scans through options on the screen. When the desired option is highlighted, the user will trigger the switch to select that option. Switch systems can replace a keyboard and/or mouse for people with motor impairments that make it difficult for them to use traditional interfaces. To communicate with a mobile device, switch systems often require some kind of interface, and a number of these interfaces for the iPad are currently available or under development:

- *RJ Cooper:* This well-known assistive technology company has developed two Bluetooth switch interfaces that work with a number of iPad augmentative and alternative communication (AAC) apps. The Bluetooth Super Switch is an interface that itself functions as a switch, and it has a port to connect a second switch. A nice feature of this interface is the size of the switch, which at five inches in diameter presents a good target for those who need it. The Bluetooth Switch Interface is a stand-alone interface with two switch ports. Both switch interfaces can be charged through a USB AC charger or by connecting them to a USB port on a computer. RJ Cooper claims a range of about 50 feet for each interface. For more information about these interfaces, visit the RJ Cooper website at www.rjcooper.com.

- *AbleNet:* The company's Blue 2 Bluetooth interface has two built-in switches (in the form of pedals in the front of the interface) that support single and dual switch access from up to 30 feet away. The interface also has two extra ports for connecting additional switches that can be used instead of the pedals. The Blue 2 runs on two AA batteries. More information about the Blue 2 is available on the AbleNet website at www.ablenetinc.com.
- *Inclusive:* The APPlicator Bluetooth switch interface has four programmable switch inputs that can be used to connect up to four wired switches. The programmable functions of this interface include 24 keyboard/mouse commands, as well as a Quick Media Mode that can be used to control music playback on the iPad. For more information about the APPlicator, visit the Inclusive website at www.inclusivetlc.com.

The four switch interfaces mentioned so far only work with specific apps that support switch access. A great resource for learning which apps have this support was created by Jane Farrall and Alex Dunn, and can be accessed at http://bit.ly/SwitchApps.

More recent, a new class of interfaces that provide more complete switch access to iOS devices has become available (with more under development):

- *Komodo OpenLab Tecla Shield:* This Bluetooth interface works with the VoiceOver screen reader to allow the user to control an iPad using either a switch or the driving controls on a powered wheelchair. The interface is compatible with any switch that uses a 3.5mm or 1/8-inch mono plug. For powered wheelchairs, it is compatible with chairs that have an environmental control unit (ECU) that follows the simple electrical transducer (SET) standard (also known as the TRACE standard). To work with the Tecla Shield, apps need to be compatible with the VoiceOver screen reader that is built into iOS. All of the built-in apps (Safari, YouTube, and Mail) have this compatibility, and more third-party apps are starting to include it as well. More information about the Tecla Shield, which was developed as an open-source project of the Komodo OpenLab in Canada, is available at http://komodoopenlab.com/tecla/tecla-for-iOS/the-basics/.

- *iPortal Accessibility:* Dynamic Controls' iPortal was developed to provide real-time information (battery status, speed, direction, etc.) to users of powered wheelchairs through the display on an iOS device. With the accessibility add-on, the iPortal also allows users of powered wheelchairs to control an iOS device with the joystick controls of their chair, a switch, or a head array. Using VoiceOver and AssistiveTouch (two of the iOS built-in accessibility features), the interface can be used to surf the web and more. To learn more about iPortal, visit www.dynamiccontrols.com/iportal/iportal-accessibility.
- *Pretorian Technologies:* Pretorian has developed two switch interfaces that provide comprehensive switch access for iOS devices: SimplyWorks and Switch2Scan. Switch2Scan allows up to four wired switches to be connected wirelessly to iOS devices via the Bluetooth interface, while the SimplyWorks allows for a combination of up to six SimplyWork switches, joysticks, or keyboards. Both interfaces feature a special iBooks mode for turning the pages of a book with a switch.
- *AbleNet Connect:* This offering from AbleNet combines a case, stereo speakers, and the switch interface in one package. The interface supports both wired and wireless switch access with scanning capabilities, has a rechargeable battery, and can be mounted with many of AbleNet's mounting solutions. More information about this interface is available on the AbleNet website at www.ablenetinc.com.

Before a switch interface can communicate with an iPad, it must first be paired with that device as follows:

1. Make sure the switch interface is turned on.
2. Go to Settings > Bluetooth.
3. Select the switch interface from the list on the iPad (you may be required to enter a pairing code with some interfaces).

With some switch interfaces that use the VoiceOver cursor to scan through the options on the screen (such as the Tecla Shield), you may have to enable VoiceOver as well. VoiceOver is a screen reader intended for people with visual disabilities, but developers have found a way to use it for switch access through its cursor that highlights items on the screen. This development highlights the need for apps to include VoiceOver accessibility, as this addition makes the app more accessible to more than one group of users (those with visual disabilities and those with motor and cognitive difficulties who rely on switch access). As with braille displays, one thing to keep in mind when using a Bluetooth switch interface is that the Bluetooth connection will drain the battery faster. If it is not possible to keep the iPad plugged into a power source while using the Bluetooth interface, it may be advisable to purchase a battery pack to extend the battery life. The Mophie battery pack that I recommended in the section on braille displays is also a good option for people who use Bluetooth switch interfaces.

Speakers and Other Accessories

Other helpful accessories include external speakers for users of alternative and augmentative communication (AAC) apps or a stylus for those who have motor impairments. RJ Cooper makes a Bluetooth speaker for the iPad, and the X-mini v1.1 is a less expensive, more lightweight option.

Many companies make a stylus for the iPad. Two of my favorites are the Pogo stylus and the Soft-Touch stylus, both of which are recommended by Apple on its accessibility site as well. The Cosmonaut stylus from Studioneat (www.studioneat.com) is shaped more like a thick crayon, and may be a good option for students with motor difficulties who need a thicker stylus. The same is true of the AluPen from Just-Mobile. For those who have difficulty with gripping a stylus, a T-shaped iPad Steady stylus is available by visiting the Etsy online store of seller shapedad (www.etsy.com/shop/shapedad).

For users who are not able to hold a stylus, the iPad MouthStick stylus (also from shapedad on Etsy) combines a mouthpiece, a pointer, and a conductive plug for hands-free use of the stylus, which is held in the mouth. Another option for hands-free use is the Capacitive HeadPointer from RJ Cooper. This pointer is worn on top of the head to allow someone with limited mobility to interact with the touch screen device thorough head movements.

Keyguards for a number of communication apps are available from a company called Lasered Pics (www.laseredpics.biz). These keyguards act as an overlay that guides the user to tap the right symbol or button on the screen, and they can be helpful for people with motor or cognitive impairments.

Updating and Syncing the iPad

Some of the features discussed in this book (Guided Access, word highlighting in Speak Selection) are only available with iOS 6, the latest version of Apple's mobile operating system. To check which version of iOS is installed on your device:

1. Open the Settings app.

Figure 2.4   Settings Icon

2. Choose General on the left side of the screen, then About on the right side.

Figure 2.5   About Option in the General Pane of Settings

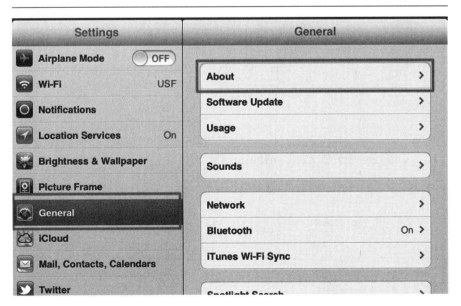

3. Scroll down until you see Version.

Figure 2.6   Information Displayed in About Pane of Settings

You can update your iPad to iOS 6 in two ways: by connecting your iPad to your computer using the included USB cable, or by doing an over-the-air update on the device itself. If you choose to update your iPad by connecting it to your computer, you will launch iTunes and follow the onscreen prompts to perform the upgrade. If a prompt does not appear, you can still update your iPad as follows:

1. Select your iPad on the right side of the iTunes window (next to the button for the iTunes Store).

Figure 2.7   Button for the iPad in iTunes

2. Choose Check for Update in the summary pane.

Figure 2.8   Summary Pane for iPad in iTunes

3. When the prompt appears, choose Download and Update to update your device to iOS 6. Once your device has been updated, you will perform the setup routine on the device as if it were a new device you purchased with iOS 6 preinstalled on it.

Starting with iOS 5, you can also update iOS from the device itself. To perform a wireless iOS update (you need to be connected to a Wi-Fi network), choose Settings > General > Software Update. If an update is available, you can tap Download and Install to start it.

Wireless syncing over Wi-Fi is also supported by iOS 6. To enable this feature, you will have to connect your iPad to your computer with a USB cable, and then in the summary tab for your device, check the box for Sync over Wi-Fi connection. Once syncing over Wi-Fi is enabled, you can sync your iPad anytime it is connected to a power source.

If you do not have access to a Wi-Fi connection, you can still use the included USB cable and iTunes to transfer content between your computer and your iPad. The iTunes software is available as a free download for Windows and comes preinstalled on the Mac. To ensure you have the latest version of iTunes, run a software update on your Mac by choosing Apple > Software Update, or download the latest version for Windows from www.apple.com/itunes/.h

Enabling Accessibility Features

There are two ways to configure the accessibility features on an iPad:

- Using iTunes to configure Universal Access on the iPad while it is connected to your computer with a 30-pin to USB or Lightning to USB cable
- Using the Settings app on the device itself, which does not require you to have the iPad connected to your computer.

To enable the accessibility features of your iPad with iTunes do the following:

1. Connect the iPad to your computer using an Apple 30-pin to USB or Lightning to USB cable.
2. Select the name of the iPad on the right side of the screen (next to the button for the iTunes Store).
3. In the summary pane, choose Configure Universal Access under Options.

Figure 2.9   Button for Configuring Universal Access Options for the iPad
in iTunes

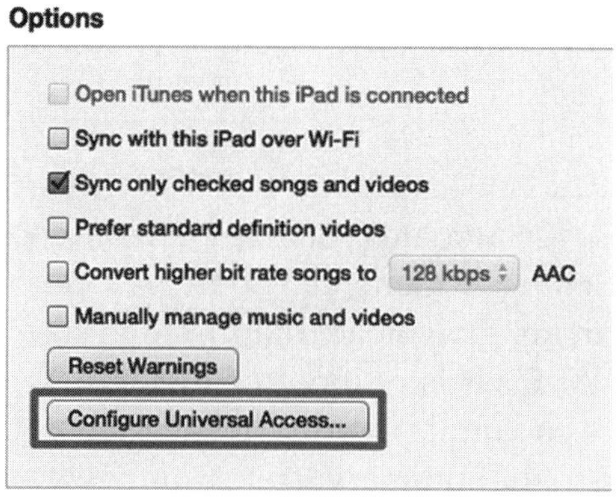

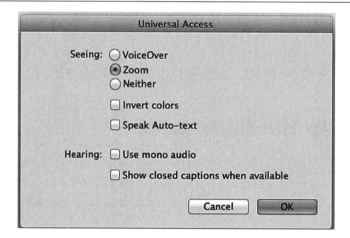

4. Select the accessibility features you want to enable and choose
OK to close the window.

Figure 2.10   Universal Access Pane in iTunes

To enable the accessibility features of your iPad with the Settings
app do the following:

1. Tap the icon for the Settings app to open it. If you are not able
to find the Settings app on one of your screens, you can search
for it using Spotlight: flick to the right or click the Home button
while on your Home Screen (the first screen), enter "settings"
in the search box, and select the Settings app from the search
results.

2. Once the Settings app launches, choose General, then Accessibility.

Figure 2.11 Accessibility Option in the General Pane of Settings

3. For Invert Colors, Mono Audio, and Speak Auto-Text, tap the On/Off switch to enable the feature. For other options such as VoiceOver and Zoom, you will need to tap the name of the

feature to access another screen where you can enable the feature and set its options (these will be discussed in more detail later in this book).

For quick access to the accessibility features of your device, you can use the Triple-Click Home option at the bottom of the Accessibility screen.

Figure 2.12   Triple-Click Home Option in Accessibility Pane of Settings

You can set this option to toggle one of the accessibility features (VoiceOver, Invert Colors, Zoom, or AssistiveTouch) when you triple-click the Home button. This is a good option if you know you will only be using one of the features most of the time. To set up Triple-Click Home as a toggle, you first need to make sure Guided Access is turned off (Accessibility > Guided Access, tap the On/Off switch), and then make sure you only have a single option selected for Triple-Click Home (as indicated by the checkmark). Guided Access is a new feature in iOS 6 for enabling a single-app mode that will be discussed in more detail in the chapter on communication apps.

Figure 2.13   Options for Triple-Click Home

If you have more than one option selected, triple-clicking the Home button will bring up a popover menu that will allow you to select the accessibility features you can enable: VoiceOver, Invert Colors, Zoom, or AssistiveTouch. A checkmark will indicate any features that are already turned on.

Figure 2.14   Accessibility Options Popover Invoked by Triple-Clicking the Home Button

This is a handy shortcut because you can bring up the menu at any time to allow you to enable or disable accessibility features without having to exit the current app or book. For example, if a student is reading a book in iBooks and wants to hear it read aloud with VoiceOver, he or she does not have to exit iBooks and open the Settings app to enable VoiceOver. By triple-clicking the Home button, the student can use the menu to quickly enable VoiceOver from within iBooks. Scan QR Code 2.1 with a QR reader app to access a video that provides an overview of the accessibility options available in iOS (the video can also be accessed at http://bit.ly/iOSAccessOverview):

QR Code 2.1
Overview of
Accessibility
Features in iOS

Starting with iOS 5, one of the major improvements for people with visual disabilities is that the Triple-Click Home option is set to toggle VoiceOver by default during setup. This means that a person who is blind can activate VoiceOver without any sighted assistance as soon as the device is out of the box and can complete the setup routine independently.

In addition to the built-in accessibility features, iOS includes other features that benefit students with a wide range of special needs. The next chapter focuses on the many learning supports built into iOS, as well as apps that provide text to speech, dictation and speech recognition, and other supports that can benefit all learners, not just those who have learning disabilities.

Practice Activities

1. Check to see what version of iOS you have installed on your iPad using one of the methods described in this chapter (using iTunes or in the Settings app on your device).
2. Update your iPad to iOS 6 using one of the methods described in this chapter. (Note: You will only be able to do an over-the-air update if you already have at least iOS 5 installed on your device).
3. With your device connected to your computer with a 30-pin to USB or Lightning to USB cable, practice enabling the Invert Colors feature (white on black display) in iTunes. Disconnect your device and use it for a few minutes with Invert Colors enabled (open a web page in Safari).
4. Plug your device back into your computer and use iTunes to disable the Invert Colors feature you enabled in the previous step.
5. With your device unplugged from the computer, practice enabling the Invert Colors feature using the Settings app. After

using your device for a few minutes (open a web page in Safari), go back into Settings and disable Invert Colors.

6. With Guided Access disabled in the Settings (General > Accessibility > Guided Access) set up the Triple-Click Home option to toggle the VoiceOver screen reader (make sure it is the only option selected for Triple-Click Home).

7. Triple-click the Home button and move your finger around the screen once VoiceOver is enabled to listen to the items on the screen as they are announced. Triple-click Home again to disable VoiceOver.

8. Set up Triple-Click Home to include Invert Colors and AssistiveTouch. Practice triple-clicking Home and turning each of those features on and off with the popover menu.

3

Learning and Literacy Supports

Some students require additional supports during reading, such as access to a dictionary where they can look up unfamiliar words or text to speech to support encoding. Both of these features are now built into the iOS software for the iPad, and they are also supported in the iBooks app students can use to read electronic books. Using iBooks also allows students to highlight, take notes, and bookmark difficult passages for review later. With Version 2, the app added support for interactive textbooks with embedded videos, photo galleries, 3D simulations, and review widgets. The embedded content can be used to provide multiple representations of difficult concepts, and review widgets can be added to the end of chapters or sections to help students check their understanding as they progress through the text.

In this chapter, educators will not only learn how to use the learning supports built into iOS and iBooks, but they will also learn how to author their own books for their students. To ensure these books do not exclude any learners, this chapter also includes a section with some best practices for authoring accessible content for iBooks. A number of third-party apps that complement the built-in iOS features, provide alternatives to iBooks, and support content area instruction are also discussed.

Universal Design for Learning (UDL) Guidelines

- *Multiple and flexible means of representation:* Text to speech (Speak Selection) allows students to access information in multiple formats (text and audio), and the built-in dictionary allows students to look up unfamiliar words as they read to help with comprehension. Apps such as iMovie and Garageband allow teachers to be creative in the way they can present information to visual and auditory learners.

- *Multiple and flexible means for expression:* Speech recognition (dictation) and audio recording apps allow students who have typing difficulties to take notes, compose emails, and more using just their voice to interact with the mobile device. Graphic organizer apps allow visual learners to express their ideas visually, and iMovie and Garageband provide options for students to show their understanding in creative ways (movies, video reflections, etc.).

- *Multiple and flexible means for engagement:* The portability of the iPad makes it ideal for problem-based learning projects that take students out of the classroom and engage them with real-world problems in their communities (interviewing community residents for oral history projects, documenting problems in their communities through video, etc.). Apps such as iMovie and Garageband also provide choices for how students document and reflect on their learning.

iOS Built-In Learning Supports and Complementary Apps

Dictionary

Checkpoint 2.1—Clarify vocabulary and symbols.

You can use the built-in iOS dictionary to select a word and get a definition. In addition to the word's meaning, you will also see its origin as well as examples of its use. Most apps support this feature, but there are a few exceptions because some apps display text in a special way that does not allow it to be selected. If the app supports text selection, you can see a word's definition as follows:

1. Tap and hold on the word briefly, until it is highlighted.
2. Tap Define to open a popover with the definition and other information about the selected word.

Figure 3.1   Popover With Define Option for the Dictionary

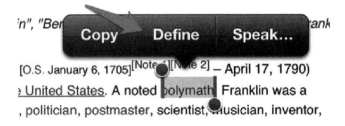

Figure 3.2   Popover Showing Definition for a Selected Word

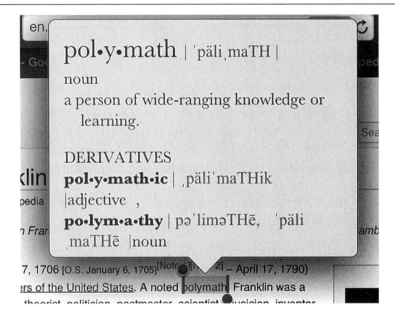

3. Tap anywhere outside the popover window to dismiss the dictionary when you are done reading the definition.

The built-in dictionary provides vocabulary help for students while making it possible for them to stay on task. Rather than having to switch apps to open a separate dictionary app when they want to look up an unfamiliar word (which may cause them to lose focus), the built-in dictionary can be opened at any time without exiting the current app. Once a they have read the definition, students can quickly return to the text and pick up right where they left off.

I prefer to use the built-in dictionary whenever possible because of its convenience, but a number of third-party dictionary apps are also available with additional features such pronunciation:

- **Dictionary.com—Dictionary and Thesaurus**

  Free (with in-app upgrades)

  This ad-supported app (you can remove the ads with an in-app upgrade) has more than two million definitions and 90,000 synonyms and antonyms. Because of its large size, this app can take several minutes to download over a Wi-Fi connection, so the developers recommend installing it on the computer with iTunes and then syncing it to the mobile device. Most of the content in the app is available even if you do not have Internet access. Along with the definitions, you get a built-in thesaurus and audio pronunciations. I would recommend purchasing the upgrade to remove the ads and minimize distractions.

- **WordWeb**

  Free (with in-app upgrades)

  WordWeb is available in two versions: the free version that has 285,000 words but no audio support, and a paid version that adds 70,000 audio pronunciations. The free version does not include any ads, which is important for minimizing distractions.

Both of these apps can be downloaded from www.pinterest.com/mlearning4all/vocabulary/.

Speak Selection

Checkpoint 2.3—Support decoding text, mathematical notation, and symbols.

Sometimes listening to the text can help a student with understanding by providing the same information in a different modality. A number of research studies provide evidence for the positive impact of text to speech on comprehension, especially for struggling readers. For example, Leong (1995) found that below-average readers' comprehension was improved by the use of text to speech, and Montali and Lewandowski (1996) found that struggling readers performed as well as average readers when text was presented in this bimodal fashion. Wise and Olson (1994) worked specifically with students identified as having reading disabilities and found that text to speech improved comprehension. More recent, Disseldorp and Chambers (2002) studied the effects of text to speech on readers of various abilities, finding an overall average of 7% improvement in comprehension, with poorer readers benefiting more than better readers. Similarly, Hecker, Burns, Elkind, Elkind, and Katz (2002) found that for college students with attention deficit disorders, the text to speech improved attention to the text (as measured by distractions during reading). More research focusing on the use of text to speech on newer devices is needed to confirm these effects seen in studies conducted before e-readers were widely available.

The Speak Selection feature in iOS allows a student to select text and have it read aloud using the same voice available with the VoiceOver screen reader for people with visual disabilities. To enable this feature do the following:

1. In the Settings app, go to General > Accessibility > Speak Selection.

Figure 3.3 Speak Selection Option in Accessibility Pane

2. Tap the On/Off switch, then use the slider to adjust the speaking rate as desired. I usually set the slider about a third of the way in (from the left), but every student is different.

Figure 3.4 Speaking Rate Slider for Speak Selection

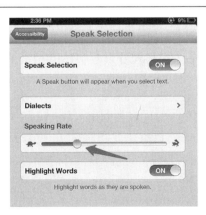

3. Tap the On/Off switch for Highlight Words. This feature can help struggling readers by making it easier for them to follow the words as they are read aloud.

Once the feature is enabled, open an app that has text, and use Speak Selection to hear the text read aloud as follows:

1. Tap and hold briefly over the text to reveal a popover menu with Speak as one of the options.
2. Use the blue handles to select the desired text. A loupe will appear as you drag the handles to help you make the selection more precise.
3. Tap Speak on the popover menu to hear the text read aloud.

Figure 3.5   Popover for Speak Selection

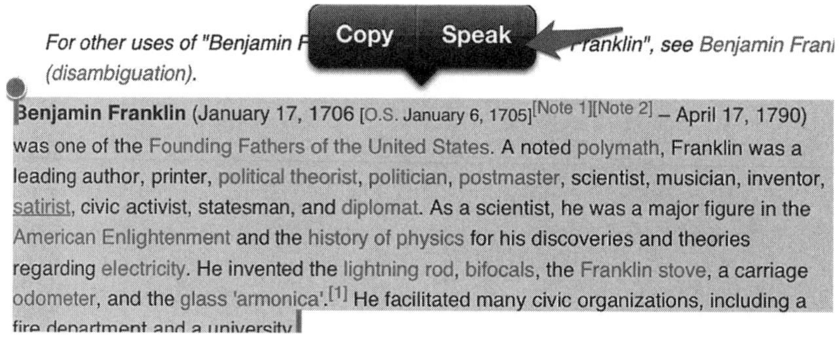

4. Tap Pause if you need to briefly stop Speak Selection. Tapping Speak again will make it pick up right where it left off before you tapped Pause.
5. To dismiss the popover menu (and stop Speak Selection), tap anywhere outside the selected text.

Like the built-in dictionary, the Speak Selection feature will work in most apps. The exceptions are apps that display the text in a special way that does not allow for it to be selected.

In addition to the built-in Speak Selection feature of iOS, a number of third-party apps for text to speech are available. These third-party apps tend to have a higher-quality voice than Speak Selection, as well as additional features such as the ability to save the text as an audio file. Some of my favorite text-to-speech apps include the following:

- NeoKate

  Free

  This app is actually one of three free text-to-speech apps from NeoSpeech (the others are NeoPaul and NeoJulie). Each app includes only one voice, which can be customized by adjusting the pitch, volume, and speaking rate. The app also supports saving the spoken text to a built-in library. For the price (free!) I have found the voice included with each of the NeoSpeech apps to be very natural sounding.

- Speak It!

  $1.99

  Speak It! features two American voices and two British voices (additional voices in a number of languages can be purchased in-app for $0.99 each). You can customize each voice by adjusting the volume and speaking rate, and you can change text size in the editing window as well. One advantage of this app is that in addition to saving to a built-in library, you can also email the text as a sound file.

- Talk to Me

  $1.99

  Very similar to Speak It! Talk to Me can speak words as you type. It has a pause feature, and it can continue to speak in the background even after you exit the app. This can be helpful if you want to listen to a long passage while working in another app.

- App Writer US

  $19.99

  While it is one of the more expensive apps on this list, App Writer is a more full-featured text editor that includes a number of other supports in addition to text to speech, such as highlighting as it speaks, word prediction, and a special font designed for those with dyslexia (the dyslexie font). Documents created in App Writer can be emailed as a text file, uploaded to Google Docs, or saved to a drop box account.

- Something to Say

  $6.99

  This text-to-speech app supports folders to allow students to save messages for later use. The appearance of the folders (color, text, and images) can be customized to make it easier for students to find the appropriate messages for a given situation. The app comes with voices from Acapela, and students can create customized voice profiles by adjusting the pitch and speaking rate of the built-in voices.

To download these apps on your iPad, visit www.pinterest.com/mlearning4all/text-to-speech/.

Spelling

Checkpoint 2.3—Support decoding text, mathematical notation, and symbols.

Students who have difficulty with spelling can improve their writing by using the built-in iOS spellchecker to identify misspelled words as they type. To enable spell checking in iOS, go to Settings > General > Keyboard and set the switch for Check Spelling to On.

Figure 3.6   Check Spelling Switch in Keyboard Pane

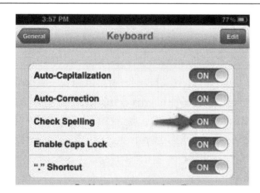

Whenever a word is misspelled it will be highlighted with a wavy red line underneath it. Tapping the highlighted word will show you alternatives for it. (You may have to choose Suggestions from a pop-over menu that appears when the word is selected).

Figure 3.7   Example of an Alternative Spelling Suggested by the Built-In iOS Spell Checker

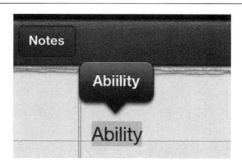

A few apps are also available with word prediction to help students who struggle with spelling:

- App Writer US

  $19.99

  As discussed in the previous section on text to speech, this app also has a word completion feature. At the time of writing, this word prediction feature also supported Spanish for English language learners.

- Abilipad

  $19.99

  This note-taking app supports word prediction and text to speech. You can hear each sentence with one of the included high-quality voices from Acapela, and you can also choose to have each word spoken as it is entered. A unique feature of Abilipad is that you can edit the keyboard and create customized layouts with bigger keys and images. Each key can represent a word or an entire phrase, and you can add a voice recording that says the contents of the key aloud when you press it. These custom keyboards can be shared with other Abilipad users.

- Typo-O HD

  $14.99

  This word prediction app has three levels of spelling correction and the ability to include the text in an email or text message. Typo-O includes a choice of four voices students can use to hear each word before adding it to a sentence.

To download these apps, visit www.pinterest.com/mlearning4all/spelling/.

Recording Apps

While the iPad has a built-in microphone, the Voice Memos app available on other iOS devices is not included with the iPad. However, a number of recording apps have similar functionality to the Voice Memos app for iPad users. Three of my favorites are the following:

- Garageband

  $4.99

  Although designed for music creation, this app also includes an audio recorder feature that can be used for recording vocals. Recordings can be synced to a computer with iTunes or shared in an email message.

- Voxie Pro Recorder

  $4.99

  This app has a simple, uncluttered design that is perfect for younger students or those with cognitive disabilities who may be easily confused by a complicated interface. The app also supports an express mode where students can start and stop a recording by shaking the device or by tapping anywhere on the screen. Recordings can be organized into categories (assignments, paper ideas, etc.), and they can be shared through email.

- Sound AMP R

  $4.99

  This app was designed to provide sound amplification for students with hearing loss, but it has a nice recording feature that I use to record lectures. One of the features I like about this app is the ability to add bookmarks at key points in the recording with a simple tap of the Add (+) button. Recordings can be shared in an email message or downloaded from a Web browser on a computer that is connected to the same Wi-Fi network.

Many of these recording apps can be used by educators and other professionals to record IEP meetings. To download the recording apps in this section, visit www.pinterest.com/mlearning4all/recording/.

Dictation

Checkpoint 4.1—Vary the methods for response and navigation.
Checkpoint 5.2—Use multiple tools for construction and composition.

Starting with the third-generation iPad, it includes a built-in dictation feature that allows students to use speech recognition to dictate their thoughts into any app that accepts text entry. This feature is available anytime the onscreen keyboard is visible. To start dictating, tap the Dictate icon (a microphone) to the left of the space bar on the onscreen keyboard.

Figure 3.8   Dictation Button on the Onscreen Keyboard of a Third-Generation iPad

Tap Done when you're done with your dictation, and your text should appear in the appropriate text box or document.

Figure 3.9   Dictation Feature in Listening Mode

You can then use the onscreen keyboard to correct any mistakes. No training to a specific user's voice is necessary for the dictation to work. You can use this feature to compose emails, text messages, brief notes, and more. You should note that dictation will only work when Internet access is available.

For users of older versions of the iPad that do not include the Dictation feature, the free Dragon Dictation app from Nuance Communications (available at www.nuancemobilelife.com) is a good alternative. This easy-to-use app works well for dictating short messages. Like the built-in Dictation feature, Dragon Dictate requires an active Internet connection to work. To create a new dictation with Dragon Dictation do the following:

1. Open the app and tap the Record button in the center of the screen (the red dot).

Figure 3.10   Dictation Button on Dragon Dictation Main Screen

2. Speak your message clearly and slowly (think of it as using your radio announcer voice).
3. Tap the screen to end your recording.
4. If you need to make a correction, tap the keyboard icon at the bottom of the screen and use the onscreen keyboard to enter the correct text.
5. When done, tap the last button in the upper-right corner and choose how you want to share your message. You can email it, post it as a status message on Twitter or Facebook, or copy and paste the text into another app for additional editing and formatting.

Figure 3.11   Options for Sharing From Dragon Dictation

6. To create another message, tap the Add (+) button on the toolbar, or to delete the current message, tap the Trash icon.

Translation Apps

Checkpoint 2.4—Promote understanding across languages.

While the Dictation feature does not have translation capabilities, several third-party apps are available that can be used for this purpose:

- Google Translate

  Free

  This app supports more than 60 languages. For many of the supported languages, you can input the text to be translated using your voice instead of by typing it, and you can also hear the translated text read aloud to make sure you have the right pronunciation.

- SayHi Translate

  $0.99

  This translation app has voice recognition and text-to-speech support for 33 languages and dialects. A nice feature of this app is the ability to share the translation as a text message, email, Tweet, or Facebook update from within the app.

- iTranslate

  Free (with in-app upgrades)

  This app has support for more than 50 languages. It includes free voices for 18 languages, with additional high-quality voices available as in-app purchases. Speech recognition for six languages is also included, along with a dictionary feature that provides suggestions for words that have multiple meanings (this feature is also only available for some languages). Additional features include auto-completion to speed up translations, a history feature to save frequently used phrases, and the ability to share translations via email, text message, or Twitter.

Translation apps can be especially helpful when working with students who are learning a new language and who often need to look up unfamiliar words and phrases in the target language. To download these apps, visit www.pinterest.com/mlearning4all/translation/.

Notes

Checkpoint 6.3—Facilitate managing information and resources.

For students with cognitive disabilities that affect memory, the Notes app provides a quick way to jot down ideas before they are forgotten. The Notes app also has a simple and easy to use interface with few options to confuse students who might not be able to use a more full-featured note-taking app. In fact, the only two options available for the Notes app are changing the font (which can be done by going to Settings > Notes) and the text size. This last option is controlled by the Large Text setting in the Accessibility settings (Settings > General > Accessibility).

To create a new note, open the Notes app and tap the Add (+) icon, and then use the onscreen keyboard to enter the desired note text and tap Done. With iCloud, notes can be updated among all your iCloud-connected devices and computers. To sync your notes with iCloud, go to Settings > iCloud, then tap the On/Off switch for Notes. You can also email or print a note by tapping the Share button in a note (printing is only supported by AirPrint compatible printers).

For those students who need a more robust note-taking app, there are several apps that support text, audio, and images for multiple representations of the information. Some favorites are listed here:

- Evernote

  Free

  Evernote is a cross-platform note-taking system students can use to collect and organize information on multiple devices. Evernote has created apps for every major mobile and desktop operating system, as well as bookmarklets for popular Web browsers that allow students to quickly take notes as they surf the Web. Notes taken on one device are automatically synced to all the other devices where students have an Evernote account. The Evernote app for iOS allows students to organize notes into notebooks, and in addition to text notes, the app supports audio memos and photo attachments.

- AudioNote

  $4.99 (Free lite version)

  This note-taking app supports synchronized audio and text. As the audio recording takes place in the background, students can type or draw notes in a notepad. During playback, they can navigate to key points of the recording either by using the audio controls or by tapping a word in the text. Notes can be shared over a Wi-Fi connection or emailed. A free version of the app with a recording time limit is also available.

- Notability

  $0.99

  Like AudioNote, Notability supports synchronized audio and text. Notes can also include photos taken with the camera or imported from the Camera Roll, drawings, and links to Web pages. Students can organize their notes according to subject, and automatic backup to Dropbox (the free online storage service) is supported. Notability can also be used to annotate PDF documents. Using the annotations tools in Notability, the teacher can provide feedback on a PDF document a student has submitted, then email the annotated document back to the student or export it to the shared Dropbox folder where the student can access it.

- Penultimate

  Free

  Now owned by Evernote, Penultimate is a handwriting app that can be used for note taking. Penultimate works much better with a stylus. You write or draw your notes on the iPad screen, and they are then stored for you in a "notebook." This is a good app for students who can use a stylus and don't have any fine motor difficulties with handwriting. Penultimate is also a good app for subjects such as math and science where a lot of graphs and diagrams are used.

To download these note-taking apps, visit www.pinterest.com/mlearning4all/note-taking/.

Graphic Organizer Apps

Checkpoint 3.2—Highlight patterns, critical features, big ideas, and relationships.
Checkpoint 6.3—Facilitate managing information and resources.
Graphic organizer or mind-mapping apps can help students with brainstorming, note-taking (especially for visual learners), and overall organization of their thoughts during the writing process.

- Inspiration Maps

  $9.99

  This is the iPad version of the popular Inspiration concept-mapping software for the computer. Like the computer version, there are two integrated views: one for creating diagrams from linked symbols that can include text and images, and an outline view that shows just the text organized in an outline. The outlines created with Inspiration Maps can be opened with other apps such as Pages to continue the writing process.

- Idea Sketch

  Free

  Like Inspiration Maps, this free app has an integrated outline view to go along with the concept maps. Students can use this app to organize their ideas for presentations or essays.

- Popplet

  $4.99

  The individual nodes for the diagrams created with this app (called popples) can include text, drawings, and images (for visual learners). These popples can be linked together to show relationships between concepts, and the finished popplets can be shared with other people through popplet.com. A free version is available, but it is limited to one popplet.

- iCardSort

  $6.99

  iCardSort allows students to visually organize information by creating a card for each idea or concept. These cards can then be organized into decks that group related items. Double-tapping a card opens a popover window where the student can enter a note to go along with that card, as well as change the background color and font.

To download these graphic organizer apps, visit www.pinterest .com/mlearning4all/graphic-organizer/.

Reading With iBooks

The e-book reader app for Apple mobile devices is called iBooks. It is not one of the built-in iOS apps, but it is available as a free download from the App Store. The iBooks app can open books in the following formats:

- *ePub,* an industry standard for e-books supported by the International Digital Publishing Forum (IDPF). ePub is the format of most of the books available for purchase on the iBookstore, but educators can also author their own ePub books with the Pages app that is part of the iWork suite for the Mac. Adobe's InDesign offers a cross-platform option for ePub authoring on Windows computers, but it is professional-level software with a steep learning curve and a significant price tag.

- *iBooks*, a new format for interactive textbooks from Apple. These interactive textbooks can include embedded videos, photo galleries, presentations, and 3D simulations to bring the content to life for students. The iBooks format is only supported on the iPad starting with Version 2 of iBooks. Educators can author their own iBooks textbooks with the iBooks Author app for the Mac. This free app can be installed from the App Store on any Mac running OS X Lion (10.7) or later.
- *PDF*, a legacy format that was originally developed for cross-platform compatibility. While iBooks can display PDF documents, the PDF format in iBooks does not support many of the interactive features discussed in this chapter. However, PDF support is still important because many older documents use this format, and PDF documents are the only ones that can be printed from iBooks with a compatible AirPrint-enabled printer.

A key difference for each format is the way in which you navigate the books. For ePub books, you go to the next or previous either by using a one-finger flick gesture to turn the page or by scrolling up or down (if the book is set to the new Scroll theme introduced in iBooks 3). To go to a different chapter or section of the book, you can tap the table of contents button at the top of the screen (you may have to tap once in the center of the screen to display the toolbar) and then select the desired chapter or section from the Contents tab.

PDF documents can be navigated in a similar way to ePub books. A one-finger flick will take you to the next or previous page, or you can use the page chooser at the bottom of the screen to go to any page in the document. When you open the table of contents, you can view the pages as thumbnails, and tapping on any thumbnail will take you to that page.

For iBooks textbooks, navigation is performed as follows:

- Flick from right to left to advance to the next chapter, or from left to right to go back. The thumbnails for the pages in each chapter will appear at the bottom in a strip.
- Tap once on a page's thumbnail and it will open full screen. To return to the thumbnail view, pinch in with two fingers.
- To open embedded content (such as a video) full screen, pinch out on it with two fingers, and then to exit the full screen view of the content, pinch in.

- To view a list of the sections in a chapter, tap the table of contents button. Tapping the name of each section will take you to the first page of the section (pinching in will return you to the table of contents for the chapter).

iBooks textbooks are displayed differently based on the orientation of the iPad. In the landscape orientation, the interactive content is emphasized. When the iPad is turned to the portrait orientation, this content is pushed to the side and the text is emphasized. Navigation in the portrait view is done by flicking up or down with one finger. Pinching in on any page will show the table of contents for the book as a list. Scan QR Code 3.1 to watch a video explaining how to navigate iBooks textbooks on the iPad (this video is also available at http://bit.ly/iBooksNavigation):

QR Code 3.1
Navigation of iBooks Textbooks

Through the iBookstore, the iBooks app provides access to a growing collection of popular books in a number of genres, including the new iBooks interactive textbooks for the iPad. Apple has partnered with textbook publishers to make a number of their textbooks available for purchase on the iBookstore at a price of $15 per textbook (free sample chapters are available for download as well).

The iBookstore also has a number of Read Aloud children's books available for purchase. These books include narration from an actual human voice, rather than synthesized speech, and the text is highlighted as the iBooks app automatically turns the pages for the reader. This highlighting feature of Read Aloud books can help new and struggling readers who sometimes have difficulty keeping their place as they read.

Reading and Study Aids in iBooks

Checkpoint 2.1—Clarify vocabulary and symbols.
Checkpoint 2.3—Support decoding of text, mathematical notation, and symbols.
Checkpoint 3.2—Highlight patterns, critical features, big ideas, and relationships.
Checkpoint 3.3—Guide information processing, visualization, and manipulation.

With books that are in the ePub and iBooks formats, the iBooks app features a number of reading supports available when text is selected:

Figure 3.12 Popover for a Selected Word in iBooks

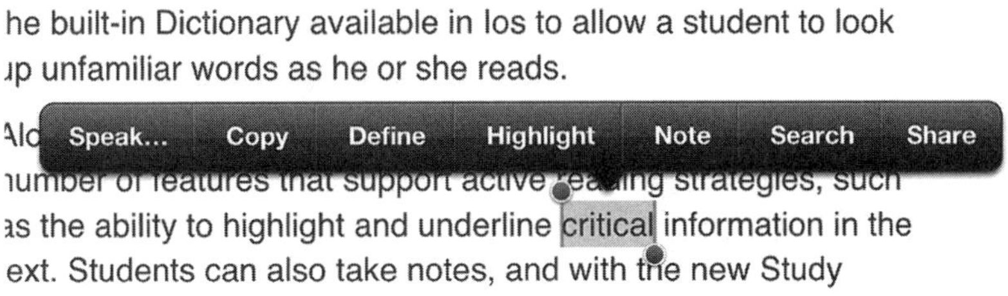

he built-in Dictionary available in Ios to allow a student to look
up unfamiliar words as he or she reads.

Alo | Speak... | Copy | Define | Highlight | Note | Search | Share

number of features that support active reading strategies, such
as the ability to highlight and underline critical information in the
text. Students can also take notes, and with the new Study

- *Speak* reads the selected text aloud (text to speech) if Speak
  Selection has been enabled in the Settings (under General >
  Accessibility > Vision). To hear the text read aloud, tap, hold
  briefly, and release over a word. When the popover menu
  appears, use the blue handles to define a selection (a loupe will
  appear as you drag to help with precision) and tap Speak. The
  Speak option in the iBooks app can benefit auditory learners,
  English language learners, and any other students who can
  benefit from having multiple representations of the information (text and audio).
- *Define* opens the built-in dictionary to allow students to look up
  an unfamiliar word. The dictionary feature of iBooks is accessed
  in the same way as the Speak feature, but when the popover
  menu appears, you may have to tap the right arrow to show
  more options. To resume reading when you are done with the
  definition, tap outside the dictionary popover window to dismiss it. For students who might lose focus when switching
  apps, having the dictionary feature built into the iBooks app
  can help them stay on task while reading.
- *Highlight* can be used to mark important passages in a book.
  Starting with iBooks 2, highlighting can be done through a simple gesture performed over the text that should be highlighted.
  The trick to this gesture is that you have to tap and hold briefly
  before dragging over the text, otherwise you will flip the page.
  If you tap the highlighted words again, you can access a popover menu to choose from one of the five available colors for the
  highlight. An underline option is also available, or you can tap
  the circle with the red line through it to remove the highlight.
  Students can use the highlighting feature to identify the main
  idea in passages or to mark important facts for review with the
  Study Cards feature that will be discussed later in this chapter.
- *Note* saves a comment about the highlighted text as a note that
  will appear on the margin of the page. To create a note, first

highlight text on the page as described previously, then tap the Note icon on the popover menu. After you've entered the note text in the text box, tap anywhere on the page and the note will be shown as an icon on the margin of the page. To edit an existing note, tap its icon on the margin to open the note, then tap inside the text box and use the onscreen keyboard to edit the note text. To remove a note, tap the highlighted text on the page and choose the circle with the red line through it (for removing a highlight). A prompt will inform you that removing the highlight will also remove the note associated with it.

- *Search* finds all the occurrences of a word or phrase in a book. To perform a search, select the desired text and choose Search from the popover menu. This will display a list showing every page where the selected word or phrase appears in the book. Along with searching within a book, the search feature also allows you do a Web search or look up a word or phrase on Wikipedia. These options are available at the bottom of the search window.

- *Share* allows students to share important passages or favorite quotes with their peers by sending them in an email or text message or by posting them on the Twitter or Facebook social networks. There is also an option to copy the selected text to work with it in another app (such as a word processing app).

For iBooks textbooks, any highlights and notes you create can be accessed as study cards that can be used for review:

1. Add a few notes to your book as described earlier in this section. For example, to test myself on key terms in a biology book, I would highlight the text in the book that defines each key term and then add a note that has the key term I want to learn.

2. Tap the Study Cards icon in the upper-left corner of the screen.

Figure 3.13   Study Cards Button

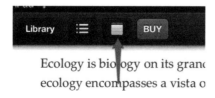

3. Rotate your iPad to the landscape orientation to display a list of highlights and notes on the left side of the screen.

4. The number to the right of each chapter indicates how many highlights or notes are in that chapter. To view those highlights and notes, tap the chapter's name, and they will appear on the right side of the screen in a My Notes area. Tapping on a highlight or note will take you to the part of the book where it was added.

5. To start your review session for a chapter, tap the Study Cards button at the top of the screen while that chapter's notes and highlights are displayed.

6. To swap the cards, swipe with one finger. The ones that have notes (not just highlights) will have a flip button in the lower-right corner. Tap this button to flip the card and reveal the key term associated with the highlighted text. Tapping a second time will flip the card again to reveal the highlighted text.

Figure 3.14   Button for Flipping Study Cards

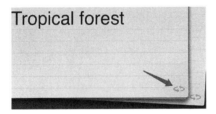

7. To shuffle the cards, tap the Study Options button in the upper-left corner (the gear icon) and set the switch for Shuffle to On.

8. When you're finished with your review and want to return to the book, tap Done in the upper-right corner of the screen to return to the My Notes view, and then tap Done a second time to return to your book.

The My Notes view is where you manage your notes and highlights for iBooks books. To delete notes or highlights, tap the Action button, then tap the circles to select the desired notes (a red checkmark will appear next to them), and choose one of the options at the top of the screen (such as Delete, or Email if you want to share the notes in an email message).

Figure 3.15　My Notes View With Options for Emailing or Deleting Notes and Highlights

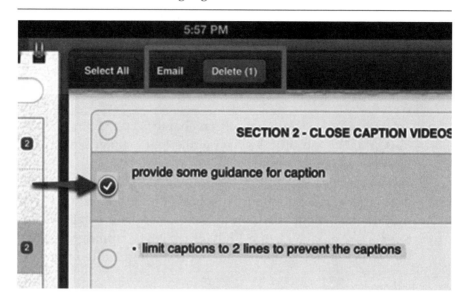

Scan QR Code 3.2 to view a short video that discusses the reading supports and study aids built into iBooks (the video is also available at http://bit.ly/iBooksStudySupports):

QR Code 3.2
Reading Supports and Study Aids of iBooks

For ePub books, a list of all your notes and highlighted passages can be accessed at any time from the book's table of contents:

1. Tap the table of contents button in the upper-left corner of the screen.

Figure 3.16　Table of Contents Button for ePub Books

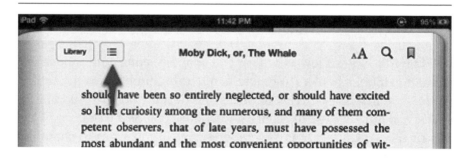

2. Select the Notes tab to display a list of your highlights and notes.

Figure 3.17 Notes Tab in Table of Contents for ePub Books

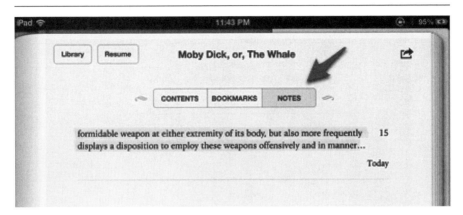

3. To remove a highlight or note, swipe over the item on the list with one finger to reveal a Delete button. Tapping this button will remove the note.

Figure 3.18 Swiping an Item in the Notes Tab Reveals a Delete Button

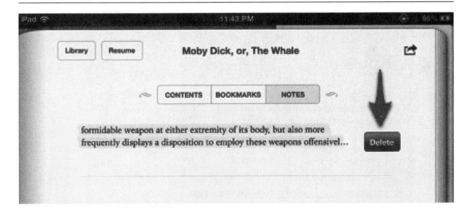

4. To share your notes in an email message, tap the action button in the upper-right corner and choose Edit Notes. Check the desired notes, then choose Share > Mail.
5. To return to your book from the table of contents, tap the Resume button in the upper-left corner of the screen. You can also just tap an item in the Notes list to go to the page where that highlight or note was added.

Interactive textbooks in the iBooks format can also include a glossary of key terms defined by the author. Glossary terms are displayed in bold in the textbook. To view the entry for a glossary term, tap the word in bold to open a popover window with the definition.

Figure 3.19   Popover With the Definition for a Glossary Entry

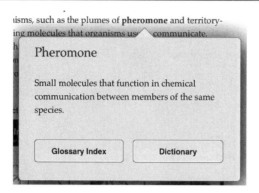

To view all the glossary entries, tap Glossary Index at the bottom of the popover window.

Figure 3.20   Glossary Index Button

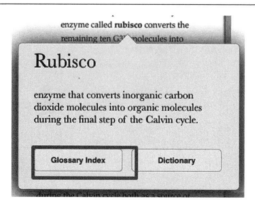

This will take you to a different screen showing a list of glossary terms on the left side of the screen and the definitions on the right if you are in landscape orientation.

Figure 3.21   Glossary Index With Entries on the Left and Definitions on
the Right

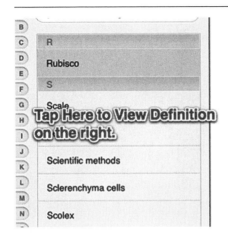

In portrait orientation, you will only see the definitions, but you can navigate by flicking up to reveal the next definition or down to reveal the previous one. To return to the book, tap Done in the upper-right corner.

While iBooks automatically keeps track of where you left off when you close the app, you can also bookmark a page that has a difficult passage you may want to reread later. These bookmarks work differently based on the format:

- With ePub books, you tap the Bookmark icon (ribbon) in the upper-right corner to add a bookmark (the icon will change to red to indicate the bookmark).

Figure 3.22   Bookmark Button for ePub Books

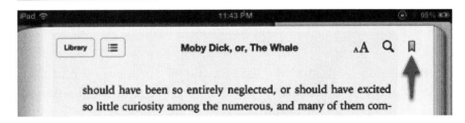

- With iBooks textbooks, you will need to tap Add Bookmark after you tap the Bookmark (ribbon) icon.

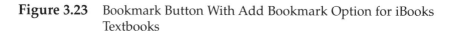

Figure 3.23   Bookmark Button With Add Bookmark Option for iBooks
Textbooks

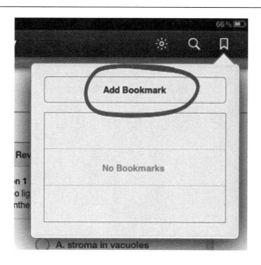

For ePub books, a list of all your bookmarks can be accessed from
the table of contents in the Bookmarks tab.

Figure 3.24   Bookmarks Tab in Table of Contents for ePub Books

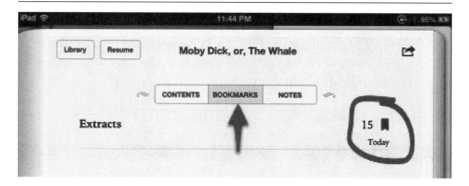

For iBooks textbooks, the list is available from the current page
when you tap the Bookmarks button. By going into the iBooks settings (Settings > iBooks), you can ensure the bookmarks you create
(as well as your highlights and notes) are synced between devices.
That way when you open the same book on another device, all of
your highlights, notes, and bookmarks will be available.

Text Display Options in iBooks for ePub

Checkpoint 1.1—Offer ways of customizing the display of information.

Since ePub was a format created to deal primarily with text, there are more options for adjusting the appearance of text for ePub documents in the iBooks app. You can adjust the text size and select different fonts (including sans-serif fonts that have been found to benefit students with dyslexia). You can also choose a different theme: a Night theme with light text on a dark background, a Scroll theme for browsing the pages by scrolling up and down with one finger like you would when browsing a long Web page in a Web browser, and a Full Screen theme for removing page borders that may be distracting to some students. To access these options, tap the text icon in the upper-right corner of the screen, then choose Themes.

Figure 3.25   Popover With Text Display Options for ePub Books

Scan QR Code 3.3 to access a video about the text display options for ePub books in iBooks (or visit http://bit.ly/ePubSupportiBooks):

For iBooks textbooks, the option to change the text size is only available when the iPad is in the portrait orientation. In that orientation, the text is emphasized by moving the interactive content to the side, where it appears as thumbnails. To change the text size when

QR Code 3.3
Text Display
Options for
ePub in iBooks

the iBooks app is in portrait view, tap the text size icon, and then tap the button on the right to make the text bigger or the button on the right to make it smaller. The text will reflow just like it does with ePub books.

Figure 3.26   Popover With Text Display Options for iBooks Textbooks

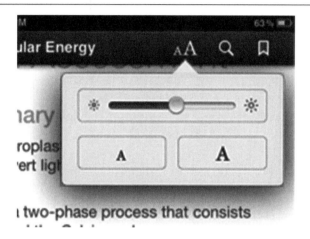

Authoring Accessible Content for iBooks

Both the iBooks and ePub formats support embedded multimedia content such as images, audio, and video clips for students who need more explicit demonstrations of difficult concepts. This rich media content can also help visual and auditory learners by providing alternative representations of the content in formats that better suit their learning styles. However, care should be taken to ensure that the use of images and other rich media does not make the content more accessible to one group of students while removing access for others. As will be discussed in more detail in the chapters focusing on visual and hearing disabilities, there are ways for authors to include images in a way that allows them to be described by the VoiceOver screen reader, and the iBooks app has support for closed-captioned videos. Since accessibility techniques for students with sensory disabilities will be addressed in their own chapters, this section focuses only on techniques for making it easier for learners to process the information in e-books. Before I turn to the specific techniques for improving accessibility, I first want to refer you to some of my favorite resources for learning how to author an ePub or iBooks textbook, in case you are new to publishing content for the iBooks app.

Apple has published an excellent article with information on how to author your first ePub document with Pages. The article also includes a link to a best practices document you can use as a template to help you get started with ePub documents in Pages. To view the article, visit http://bit.ly/AppleePubBestPractices.

For iBooks Author, the Department of Journalism at Emerson College has created an excellent video tutorial series focusing on every step of the authoring process. By following along with these tutorials, you should be able to author your first iBooks book. To view the tutorials, visit http://bit.ly/EmersonTutorials.

Once you have become familiar with the steps for authoring your first ePub book or iBooks interactive textbook, take some time to make sure the content is accessible by incorporating the techniques I discuss in the following sections into your authoring workflow.

Ensure Legibility

Before students can process information, they must be able to perceive it. Providing text in a way that makes it difficult to see will take additional effort from the reader, effort that could be better put to use for making sense of the information. While iBooks supports a reading view with text resize options for iBooks textbooks when the iPad is in the portrait orientation, a similar option is not available when the iPad is in the landscape orientation. To ensure your text is legible in this orientation, I recommend the following guidelines:

- Use a text size of at least 18.
- Select sans-serif fonts in iBooks Author. These are fonts without the extra ornamentation at the end of strokes. These fonts are easier to read for people with dyslexia. Select the appropriate font using the Format Bar rather than the Fonts window in iBooks Author to make sure your font is iPad-compatible.
- Be careful with the use of the colors red and green. Many people (males more than females) are not able to see these colors. When creating hyperlinks, a color such as blue may be easier to see for those with color vision difficulties.
- Use left justification for text. The iBooks Author templates have the body text set to left justification by default, and I recommend not changing it to full justification to avoid the jagged edges on the right side of paragraphs. Full justification can add extra gaps between the words, and these gaps can cause problems for people with dyslexia.
- Limit the use of italics. Italic text can make it difficult for readers with dyslexia to make out the letters. A better way to highlight information **is to make it bold**.

Provide an Overview

Checkpoint 3.2—Highlight patterns, key features, big ideas, and relationships.

Each iBooks textbook can include an introductory video when it opens. This video is a good opportunity to provide an overview of the content for the reader. As with any other video in your iBooks textbooks, make sure the introductory video is closed-captioned, and try to keep it brief (no more than one minute) to keep the file size for the iBook file manageable.

To add an introductory movie, select Intro Media from the sidebar in iBooks Author, then drag your video from your hard drive and drop it on top of the media placeholder.

Create a Glossary for Key Terms

Checkpoint 3.2—Highlight patterns, key features, big ideas, and relationships.

With iBooks Author, you can add a glossary of key terms to your iBooks textbooks. The glossary can be helpful for pointing out critical

QR Code 3.4
Adding a
Glossary Term
in iBooks
Author

information to students. Combined with the study cards in the iBooks app, the glossary can also be a valuable study aid for any student. These study cards are flashcards students can flip over to reveal the definition for each key term included in the glossary. To learn how to add a glossary in iBooks Author (as well as how to use the glossary with the study cards feature in the iBooks app), scan QR Code 3.4 to view a video tutorial (or visit http://bit.ly/iBooksGlossary).

Include Knowledge Checks With the Review Widget

Checkpoint 3.3—Guide information processing, visualization, and manipulation.

QR Code 3.5
Creating
a Review
Widget in
iBooks Author

Checkpoint 5.3—Build fluencies with graduated levels of support for practice and performance.
Checkpoint 6.4—Enhance capacity for monitoring progress.

In iBooks Author, you can add a review widget at the end of each chapter or section to allow students to check their understanding before moving to the next chapter or section. Doing well in these short assessments can also be motivating to reluctant readers.

To learn how to create a review widget in iBooks Author, please watch the video by scanning QR Code 3.5 or visit http://bit.ly/ReviewWidget.

Use Styles to Structure the Content

Checkpoint 3.3—Guide information processing, visualization, and manipulation.

You should take the needs of people with cognitive disabilities into consideration by splitting long documents into more manageable sections with headings, subheadings, and other styles. The document structure should be created with the Styles menu in Pages or iBooks Author (depending on the format), rather than by selecting text and making it bold and larger. Scan QR Code 3.6 to view a video focusing on styles and how to add them in either iBooks Author or Pages (or visit http://bit.ly/DocStructure).

QR Code 3.6 Using Styles to Add Structure to Documents

For ePub books, the use of styles will also allow Pages to automatically create a table of contents for the e-book when it is exported as an ePub file. To customize the appearance of the table of contents, do the following:

1. Open the Inspector by clicking the button in the toolbar or by choosing View, then Show Inspector.

Figure 3.27 Inspector Button

2. In the Table of Contents (TOC) pane, check the boxes next to the styles that should appear in the table of contents when the document is opened in iBooks. The topmost style selected in the TOC pane will be used to create chapters. The other items that are selected in the pane will be indented underneath the chapters in the exported table of contents.

Figure 3.28   Table of Contents (TOC) Pane in Document Inspector

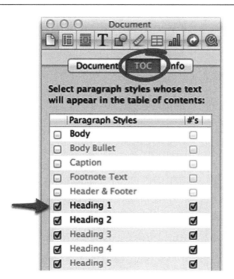

3. To hide/show page numbers for any style in the table of contents, check the box to the right of that item.

Other Reading and Authoring Apps for iOS

E-Reader Apps

Checkpoint 1.1—Offer ways of customizing the display of information.
Checkpoint 1.3—Offer alternatives for visual information.
Checkpoint 2.1—Clarify vocabulary and symbols.
Checkpoint 2.3—Support decoding text, mathematical notation, and symbols.

In addition to iBooks, a number of third-party reading apps are available for iOS. These apps usually link to an online bookstore where the reader can purchase additional books (and in some cases magazines). The support for accessibility in these third-party apps will vary. For example, not all of them fully support the VoiceOver screen reader.

- Kindle

  Free

  I often use this app because Amazon has a larger selection of books than iBooks. The app has support for word lookup in a dictionary, highlights, and notes, and a few text display options (text size, line height, and background color). While the app has some VoiceOver support, you are not able to use VoiceOver to read the text because of licensing restrictions from publishers.

- Nook

  Free

  This reading app from Barnes and Noble has many of the same features as the Kindle app (highlights, notes, dictionary, and customizable text). Like the Kindle app, it lacks support for text to speech.

- Google Play Books

  Free

  Google Play Books has the standard set of features for many of these apps (text display options, notes, highlights, etc.) as well as one unique feature: a translate option that can be helpful to English language learners. To use this feature, select any text and choose Translate from the popover menu. Translation for more than 30 languages is supported. While Google Play Books does not include built-in text to speech, it does support the VoiceOver screen reader.

- Blio

  Free

  This reading app from K-NFB supports both VoiceOver and text-to-speech voices. However, the voices have to be purchased in-app for $9.99 each. With the text-to-speech voices, the text is highlighted as the voice reads it aloud.

- Audible

  Free

  This audio book app provides access to more than 100,000 digital audiobooks available at Audible.com. Unlike the other book apps on this list, Audible does not use text to speech, but a recording of a narrator. For many titles, this narrator is the author of the book. The Audible app not only provides books in an audio format for people with visual disabilities, it is also compatible with the VoiceOver screen reader many of them use.

- Read2Go

  $19.99

  Bookshare members can use this app to access more than 140,000 e-books. Through a special grant from the U.S. Department of Education, any student who has a disability that makes it difficult to read a printed book can qualify for Bookshare services. This is not only students with visual disabilities, but also students who have physical disabilities that make it difficult to turn a page in a book and students with learning disabilities, such as dyslexia, that make it difficult to process information. All that is needed to qualify for Bookshare services is proof of the disability from a qualified professional (a family doctor, special education teacher, or in the case of learning disabilities, a school psychologist). For Bookshare books, the Read2Go app provides text to speech with high-quality Acapela voices and highlighting as the text is read aloud. It also has many text display options for adjusting the font size, text color, background, reading speed and more.

- Learning Ally

  Free

  Formerly known as Recordings for the Blind and Dyslexic, Learning Ally is a membership service that provides access to a library of more than 70,000 audiobooks read by real people rather than a computer voice. Membership is $99 a year, and it requires proof of a print disability (such as a learning disability, a visual impairment, or any kind of physical disability that makes it difficult to handle a book). The Learning Ally Audio app has options for changing the speaking rate, bookmarking important passages, and navigating by chapter or page number. The app is also compatible with the VoiceOver screen reader.

To download these e-book reader apps on your mobile device, visit www.pinterest.com/mlearning4all/reading/.

Book Apps

Checkpoint 2.5—Illustrate through multiple media.
Checkpoint 5.1—Use multiple media for communication.

The distinction between an e-book and a book app is sometimes a difficult one to make. Perhaps the easiest way to distinguish between the two is by their source: Book apps are purchased from the App Store just like other iOS apps, while e-books are purchased from an online bookstore such as the iBookstore from Apple or the Kindle store from Amazon. Book apps also tend to have additional interactivity that has been programmed by the developer, while e-books are limited to the features supported by the app used to purchase and display them. The additional interactivity can make book apps more immersive and engaging for some students, but the custom interfaces used in these apps can sometimes confuse readers with cognitive disabilities or provide too much stimulus or distractions for others. Support for the accessibility features (such as VoiceOver) is also inconsistent for many book apps. A few of the book apps allow students to record their own voice as they read. This is one of the key features that I often look for in these apps, as it can provide students with additional opportunities to build their fluency by listening to themselves read aloud.

A few of my favorite book apps are as follows:

- The Cat in the Hat–Dr. Seuss

  $3.99

  This title is from the Oceanhouse Media series of Dr. Seuss books. To promote reading in young children, individual words are highlighted as the story is read aloud and words zoom up when pictures are touched. The app has three reading modes: Read it to Me allows children to listen to the narrated story with words highlighted as they read, Read it Myself allows them to read the book in traditional form, and Autoplay automatically reads the book and turns the pages for younger children. The recommended age for this app is three to six years.

- I Like School

  Free

  Part of the "I Like" series for children ages 0–6, this app allows parents to customize the story by recording it in their own voice. Parents can turn on word highlights to have the text be highlighted as the story is read aloud, and they can also include picture highlights to help with learning new objects. With these highlights activated, the child can tap an image to hear a description in the parent's voice that helps him or her learn the object.

- Milly, Molly, and the Bike Ride HD

  $2.99

  The Milly and Molly series of book apps for the iPad from Kiwa Media relate the adventures of two little girls from different ethnic backgrounds. In this one, Milly and Molly remind themselves of the time when distractions interrupted their bike ride to Grandma's but they still made it on time. With the books in this series, students can tap any word to have it spoken aloud or spelled. They can also select Auto Play to hear the included narration, which is available in other languages such as Spanish, French, Japanese, and Mandarin Chinese (varies by app). A My Narration feature allows students to record and play back their own recording of the story, and each page has a paint mode for those reluctant readers who are on the artistic side.

- Shakespeare in Bits

  Free (Note: the app is free, but individual works need to be purchased for $14.99 each).

  Shakespeare In Bits is a series of apps from MindConnex. With these apps, students not only have access to the unabridged text of many of Shakespeare's works, but a number of other supports: inline translation to help students understand difficult words and phrases, animations with an audio soundtrack for auditory and visual learners (with recordings from well-known actors), character biographies and relationship maps to help students keep track of the interrelationships in each work, and integrated analysis and study notes for exam preparation.

To download these book apps, visit http://pinterest.com/mlearning4all/reading-book-apps/.

Book Authoring Apps

Checkpoint 5.2—Use multiple tools for construction and composition.
Checkpoint 7.1—Optimize individual choice and autonomy.
Checkpoint 7.2—Optimize relevance, value, and authenticity.
A number of book authoring apps provide an alternative way for students to show what they have learned using images, audio, and video. A few of the apps I have included in this section support recorded speech, allowing students to create their own read aloud books where another student can read the text and hear the corresponding audio recorded by a classmate at the same time.

- Book Creator for iPad

  $4.99

  This app creates books in ePub format that can be opened with iBooks, emailed to friends and family, or even submitted to the iBookstore. The books created with this app can include text, images, videos, and audio (either recorded speech or music). In my opinion, this is the easiest of the book authoring apps to learn and use, and I recommend it for working with young children or those with cognitive disabilities. Laying out each page is made easier with the built-in guides and snap positioning, and images can be moved and resized right on the screen using handles.

- Creative Book Builder

  $3.99

  Unlike Book Creator, with this app you don't really layout a book, but rather build its elements using a series of menus and dialogue windows. While the interface is fairly clear, I thought all the dialogue windows and menus could present a challenge to someone with a cognitive disability. Having said that, this app has some nice features such as support for video files, integration with Google Docs, and the ability to include images with attribution from the Web (to model good digital citizenship).

- Pictello

  $18.99

  Pictello is an easy way to create a talking book from your photos taken with your device's camera. For each page in the book, you add an image, type in text, and select to have the text read aloud by a text-to-speech voice or record your own audio. Books can be shared by syncing to a computer with iTunes, or through a Pictello sharing server where they can be downloaded by another Pictello user with a special code (this requires creating a free sharing account).

- StoryKit

  Free

  This free app can be used to create storybooks with text, images, recorded audio, and drawings. Stories can be shared through a special StoryKit server that provides a private Web address students can email to their teacher. The one tip I have for this app is to not include an image, a drawing, and text on the same page, as it will be difficult to see all three. An image and text, or a drawing by itself should be fine, even if you add audio to the page.

To download these book authoring apps, visit: http://pinterest.com/mlearning4all/reading-authoring-apps/.

iWork for iOS

Checkpoint 5.2—Use multiple tools for construction and composition. Checkpoint 7.2—Optimize relevance, value, and authenticity.

Apple has created iOS versions of its popular iWork productivity software for the Mac. While the iOS versions of Pages, Keynote, and Numbers provide most of the tools students need to do their work on the go, these apps are optimized for mobile devices. However, each of these apps is compatible with its Mac counterpart, and iCloud makes it simple to transfer documents between the two. iWork for iOS also supports importing Microsoft Office documents, and AirPrint can be used to print wirelessly to a compatible printer.

Like the Mac version, iWork for iOS consists of three apps that can be purchased separately for $9.99 through the App Store: Pages for word processing and page layout, Keynote for presentations, and Numbers for spreadsheets. When paired with an Apple wireless keyboard (or any case that includes a Bluetooth keyboard), Pages is a powerful note-taking and word processing app that allows students to work on their writing anywhere they can take their devices. With Keynote, students can create presentations that combine text with images taken with their device's camera, for learning that engages multiple modalities. A separate app called Keynote Remote ($0.99) makes it possible to control a presentation on an iPad from an iPhone or iPod touch. To use Keynote Remote from another iOS device, you must first allow access by choosing Settings > Advanced > Remotes in the Keynote app on your iPad. The third iWork app, Numbers, can be used as a data-collection and analysis tool for math and science activities. Each app comes with a tutorial document for help with getting started.

The iWork apps can be used to support project-based learning activities that extend learning beyond the four walls of the classroom.

For example, students can use the Numbers app as a research log that allows them to collect information out in the community. The Keynote app provides a way for students to show what they have learned about a particular topic in an engaging and visually appealing way by combining text with images taken with their mobile devices. With Pages, students can create flyers, questionnaires, and other documents to support their project-based activities.

iMovie and Garageband for iOS

Checkpoint 5.2—Use multiple tools for construction and composition.
Checkpoint 7.1—Optimize individual choice and autonomy.
Checkpoint 7.2—Optimize relevance, value, and authenticity.
Checkpoint 9.3—Develop self-assessment and reflection.

iMovie and Garageband for iOS are multimedia authoring apps that provide students with alternatives for showing their understanding of a topic. With iMovie for iOS, students can fully express their creativity through digital storytelling projects that combine video, photos, music, and narration. Garageband for iOS can be used to record podcasts about events, people, and places that are important to students. Using the built-in microphone and camera on their devices, students can also use these apps to record reflections about the topics discussed at school. The possibilities for multimedia projects with iMovie and Garageband for iOS are only limited by the teacher and students' imagination. Both iMovie and Garageband are available through the App Store for $4.99 each.

Early Literacy Apps

Checkpoint 2.2—Clarify syntax and structure.
Checkpoint 5.2—Use multiple media for communication.

In addition to the many book apps for young children, a number of apps provide practice in the basic skills needed to develop early literacy (including letter knowledge and phonemic awareness):

- Interactive Alphabet

  $2.99

  Each flashcard in this app is meant to be a toy with interactivity to keep children engaged while they learn phonics. In addition to the interactive element, each flashcard has the letter, a word that begins with that letter and the matching sound. A special Baby Mode auto advances the cards every 15 seconds.

- ABC PocketPhonics

  Free

  PocketPhonics teaches the sounds for all the letters in the alphabet as well as over 30 letter sounds like "sh and "ch." In addition to letter tracing activities, this app has a number of blending (combining a series of separately spoken phonemes to form a word) and segmentation (break a word apart into its separate sounds) activities.

- SuperWhy!

  $2.99

  With this app from PBS Kids, the child can play along with each of the main characters from the PBS TV series (Alpha Pig, Princess Presto, Wonder Red, and Super Why!) while practicing the alphabet, rhyming, spelling, writing, and reading. The app is intended for kids ages three to six.

- Intro to Letters

  $4.99

  Based on the Montessori method, this app includes a number of interactive activities to help children recognize, pronounce, and write lowercase letters, capital letters, and phonograms (letters or letter combinations that make a single sound). Children can hear the letter sound or name aloud as they trace it, hear the letter sound followed by the letter name, or record themselves saying each letter sound or name.

- Little Speller

  Free

  This app helps children learn spelling as they play an interactive game. For each word, a narrator says the letters as they are placed into the correct order to spell the word, then repeats the letters after the word is spelled for reinforcement. The app can be customized in a few ways: you can add your items with images taken with your device's camera, and you can record your own voice for each item.

- StoryPals

  $19.99

  This is a story comprehension app for iPad that features more than 20 original stories with interactive illustrations. Children can read the stories independently, or listen to them using the built-in text-to-speech voices from Acapela (with word highlighting). They can also record themselves reading each story for practice and listen to the recordings at a later time. To check their compression, each story includes a quiz focusing on 10 WH questions (who, what, where, etc.). A nice feature of this app is that you are not limited to the included stories. As a parent or teacher, you can create new stories and add illustrations with the included illustration elements (backgrounds, people, animals, and objects) or your own photos, as well as your own quizzes.

- Kids Journal

  $1.99

  This app encourages children to be reflective learners. It provides a space where they can write about their day and even include photos of the day's events. Each child can have her or his own login to separate the journal entries, and journals can be exported into files that can be read by iBooks and other apps.

To download these early literacy apps, visit http://pinterest.com/mlearning4all/early-literacy/.

Apps for Content Area Instruction

The apps in this section provide supports for subject areas such as math, social studies, and science. The list for each content area is not exhaustive because of space constraints, but it includes a diverse selection covering many of the types of apps available for each category.

Math

Checkpoint 2.5—Illustrate through multiple media.
Checkpoint 5.3—Build fluencies with graduated levels of support for practice and performance.

In addition to the built-in Calculator app, I also like Talking Calculator ($1.99, http://bit.ly/TalkingCalc) because it speaks the entered numbers, answers, and formulas aloud. This app is also compatible with the VoiceOver screen reader and has a high contrast mode (black on yellow), two features that are helpful for students with low vision (Checkpoint 1.3—Provide options for visual information).

The following apps provide children with multiple opportunities to practice basic math skills (counting, basic arithmetic, etc.). Using these apps, children can build their math skills using their mobile devices at home as a complement to their work at school.

- Cute Math

  $1.99

  This app for children up to five years of age provides practice with counting, sequencing, and simple addition and subtraction.

- Coin Math

  $1.99

  Students who struggle with numbers can learn how to recognize, count, add, and make change for U.S. coins with this app. The app includes voice instructions for younger learners.

- Pizza Fractions

  Free/$0.99

  This is a set of three apps that provide practice with fractions. With the first app (Beginning with Simple Fractions), an animated chef asks students to choose the correct fraction of pizza shown. The remaining apps in the series focus on more advanced skills, such as reducing fractions, finding equivalent fractions, and comparing simple fractions.

- Motion Math HD

  $2.99

  This game combines kinesthetic learning and practice with fractions, percentages, and decimals. Students answer each question by tilting their devices and placing a falling star in the correct spot on a number line. Each time the star is placed correctly on the number line it blasts off and gets closer to returning to its home in a far-away galaxy.

- MathBoard

  $4.99

  MathBoard is a multiple choice quiz generator that provides practice with basic arithmetic and one-step equation problems (e.g., 6+X=12, 5x=25). As a students take the quiz, they can work out the problem in a small scratch work area below it. Quizzes can be saved for review at a later date, and a problem solver is built-in to show students the required steps for solving each problem.

- Math Bingo

  $0.99

  The objective of the game is to get a pattern of five bingo bugs in a row by solving addition, subtraction, multiplication, and division problems.

- Algebra Touch

  $1.99

  With this app, students can manipulate and solve single variable algebraic equations using drag and drop to move terms from one side to another and tapping to factor or solve.

For math instruction, the "flipping" model is gaining popularity. In its simplest form, a flipped classroom is one where the teacher provides videos for homework (either ones that are already available online or ones he or she has created to address the student's unique learning needs), while traditional homework is done in class. The idea is that it is more beneficial for the student to work out the problems in class where the teacher can be there to answer questions and provide other support.

- Khan Academy

  Free

  Students can use this app to watch math video tutorials from Khan Academy on their mobile devices. An advantage of using the app is that students can download the tutorials to their mobile devices and watch them offline even if there is no Internet connection. Each video also has subtitles for those who need the text representation of the content, and these subtitles are used for navigation to any point in a video (clicking the time-coded subtitle will start playback at that point in the video).

- Explain Everything

$2.99

Although not intended as a math app, this screen recording app can be used by the teacher to create video tutorials similar to the ones available from Khan Academy. Students can use the app to record their own tutorials for peer tutoring activities where they teach the math concepts to their peers to learn them better themselves.

- Educreations

Free

Educreations is a whiteboard app with recording capabilities. Tutorials created with this app can be hosted on the Educreations .com Web site with a free account.

To download the math apps mentioned in this section, visit http://pinterest.com/mlearning4all/math/.

Science

Checkpoint 2.5—Illustrate through multiple media.
Checkpoint 3.2—Highlight patterns, critical features, big ideas, and relationships.
Checkpoint 3.3—Guide information processing, visualization, and manipulation.

The apps I selected for this section provide educators with alternatives for showing multiple representations of science content, whether it is the inside of a frog, the night sky, or the elements.

- Frog Dissection

$3.99

With this app, students can dissect a virtual specimen as an alternative to a real frog dissection. They can use the included virtual dissection tools and detailed instructions to complete the procedure. Once dissection is complete, the frog's organs are exposed for further study through 3D images that help students visualize the internal organs.

- Planets

  Free

  This free astronomy app has 2D and 3D views of the night sky. In the 3D planetarium-style view, students can move their devices and see a close representation of what the sky outside looks like. A visibility chart shows the best time for seeing each planet in the sky, and the app includes basic information for each planet as well as links to their entries on Wikipedia.

- NASA

  Free

  The official app is a great way for students to access NASA content, including high resolution images from space, on-demand videos, live-streaming of NASA TV, and current NASA mission information. The app requires an active Internet connection.

- Star Walk

  $4.99

  This augmented reality app labels all the stars, constellations, and satellites in the night sky. Students can use the app to track the International Space Station (ISS), or to find out what constellation is visible from their community.

- The Elements for iPad

  $13.99

  The Elements is an interactive periodic table of elements. For each element, there is a page showing not only an image of the element, but a 3D rendering students can manipulate with their fingers. On the right, there is information such as the atomic radius, structure, weight, density, and more. One thing to be aware about is that this app takes up a lot of storage because of all the high resolution and 3D content.

To download the science apps mentioned in this section, visit http://pinterest.com/mlearning4all/science/.

Social Studies

Checkpoint 2.5—Illustrate through multiple media.
Checkpoint 3.2—Highlight patterns, critical features, big ideas, and relationships.

Checkpoint 6.3—Facilitate managing information and resources.

Many of the apps in this section provide ways for students to have reference information at their fingertips so that they don't have to spend their energy trying to memorize isolated facts and can instead focus on building an understanding of the concepts. Apps such as Stack the States and Stack the Countries provide additional practice in a fun format.

- Stack the States/Stack the Countries

  $0.99 and $1.99

  The object of these games is to build a stack of states/countries that reaches the checkered line to win each level. To drop a state/country on top of the stack, the student has to answer a question about it. In addition to the game play, each app includes interactive maps and flashcards with information about each state or country.

- Articles

  $4.99

  This app presents Wikipedia articles in an interface that should be familiar to most students who use mobile devices, as it resembles the built-in Safari Web browser. The benefit of using a dedicated Wikipedia reader like this is that the interface has fewer distractions.

- MyCongress

  Free

  The developers describe MyCongress as a portal to detailed information about the U.S. Congress, including each member's Open Congress profile with contact information so that students can write to their representatives.

- Google Earth

  Free

  The iOS app allows students to explore the same global satellite and aerial imagery available in the desktop version of Google Earth, including high-resolution imagery for more than half of the world's population and a third of the world's landmass. Additional features include a Panoramio layer showing high-resolution geolocated photos from around the world, as well as geolocated Wikipedia entries.

To download the social studies apps mentioned in this section, visit http://pinterest.com/mlearning4all/social-studies/.

I was originally going to include an app for the U.S. constitution on this list, but I think students would get more out of downloading one of the free book versions of the constitution available from the iBookstore. The book version will allow students to take advantage of the many reading and study aids available in iBooks (highlighting, underlining, notes, and study cards, for example). The study cards feature would be especially helpful for any kind of review of the kinds of information students need to remember in social studies courses: key dates, people, and places.

Another helpful app for this kind of review is Evernote Peek (Free, www.evernote.com/peek/), an app that works with the iPad Smart Cover. With Evernote Peek, the student can create a flashcard with both a hint and the answer. The student can then fold back part of the Smart Cover for the hint, and then lift the rest of the cover to reveal the answer. The app now includes a virtual cover feature that does the same thing without the use of the Smart Cover (a swipe up on the screen reveals the hint at first, then the rest of the flashcard with the answer).

iTunes U

In addition to the many apps available in the App Store, iTunes U is a great source of free content from many of the world's best universities, museums, and other educational institutions. At my university, the University of South Florida, we have developed a collection called Lit2Go (also available on the Web at http://etc.usf.edu/lit2go/) that provides high-quality recordings of out of copyright content such as the works of William Shakespeare, Edgar Allan Poe, Mark Twain, and more. This audio content, which can be downloaded as MP3 files from iTunes U, can benefit auditory learners reading the works of these authors.

Apple has created a free iTunes U app to help students manage the content available through iTunes U on their mobile devices. The iTunes U app also provides access to many online courses developed and taught by professors at leading universities. Like other online courses, these courses can include announcements, assignments, and a variety of materials selected by the instructors (recommended apps, iBooks textbooks, movies, presentations, and more). With the iTunes U app's subscription feature, students can sign up to be notified when new content is available in a course.

To subscribe to a course with the iTunes U app, do the following:

1. Launch the app and choose Catalog at the top of the screen.

Figure 3.29   Catalog Button in iTunes U App

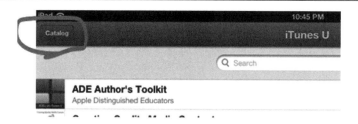

2. Use the tabs at the bottom of the Catalog to view the available content in different ways: Featured for content spotlighted by Apple, Top Charts for popular content. A search feature is also available.
3. Once you have found a course that interests you, tap its thumbnail or name to open it, then choose Subscribe Free. The course will then appear in your Library.

Figure 3.30   Subscribe Button for iTunes U Course

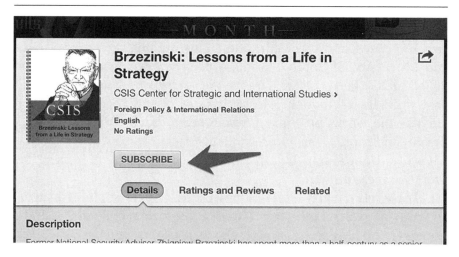

Once the course has been added to your Library, tap its thumbnail to open it, then use the tabs on the right side to choose Materials for a list of the items available in the course (movies, audio files, documents, etc.). To download any of the available items to your device, tap the download icon to the right of its description.

Figure 3.31 Download Button for Item in iTunes U Course

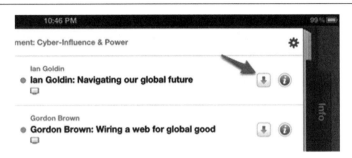

A nice feature of the iTunes U app is the ability to view any notes, bookmarks, or highlights you add to ePub books or iBooks textbooks while reading them in the iBooks app. Tapping the Notes tab will show you a list of these items arranged by date, with the latest ones at the top. You can also tap Add (+) to create a course note that is only visible in the iTunes U app.

The iTunes U app supports closed-captioning for any video that includes them. To turn on the captions for iTunes U videos, choose Settings > iTunes U, and tap the On/Off switch to enable closed-captioning support.

Practice Activities

1. Open the Safari app and go to one of your favorite Web sites. The only requirement is that the Web site have some text that you can select. Double-tap a word to see a definition, then select a longer block of text and use the Speak Selection feature to hear the text read aloud (Note: Speak Selection must be enabled in the Settings, under Accessibility).

2. Install one of the free NeoSpeech apps (NeoKate, NeoPaul, or NeoJulie) and practice entering some text and listening to it with the text to speech.

3. Open the Notes app and use Dictation on your iPad (if it supports this feature) to create a brief message. If your device does not support dictation, install Dragon Dictation and practice dictating a short message and using copy and paste to add it into a new note in the Notes app.

4. Install the free Evernote app and practice adding a brief note as both text and audio (add the voice recording of the text to your note as an attachment).

5. Install the free version of AudioNote and create a new note where you recite the first few paragraphs from the Wikipedia entry for your country as you take text notes. When you're finished, practice navigating to different points in the recording by tapping on your text notes.

6. Install the free Idea Sketch app and create a concept map of the notes you took in the previous step. Email this concept map to yourself.

7. Open the iBooks app and begin reading the free Winnie the Pooh e-book (this book is in ePub format). Practice going to the next or previous page using the one-finger flick gesture, then go to a different part of the book using the page chooser at the bottom of the screen.

8. Use the table of contents to quickly go to the end of the book and find out more about the author.

9. Change some of the text display options, such as the text size and font, then turn on the Night theme and read a few pages of the book. How does that feel? Try out the Sepia theme and enable the Full Screen mode. What changed?

10. Locate your favorite phrase in the first chapter of the book and highlight it, and then use the Dictionary feature to look up a word in that sentence and write a definition in your own words using a Note.

11. Practice changing the color of the highlight you created in the previous step, then making it into an underline.

12. Remove the note you created in step 10. (Hint: Remove the highlight.)

13. Select the same phrase and use Speak Selection to hear it read aloud. Go to the Settings app and change the speaking rate for Speak Selection to its maximum value. (Hint: General > Accessibility > Speak Selection) Now go back to the book and have the text read aloud again. Could you understand it? Go back to Settings and change the speaking rate back to your desired value.

14. Bookmark your favorite page in the book, go to a different point in the book, and use the table of contents to return to the bookmarked page.

15. Return to the table of contents and remove the bookmark you created in the previous step. (Hint: Go to the Bookmarks tab

and use a one-finger swipe gesture for the bookmark you want to remove.)

16. Search for the word "Winnie" in the book. How many times does it appear in the book. (Hint: Scroll to the bottom of the search results.)

17. Download the ePub best practices document from Apple (available at http://support.apple.com/kb/HT4168) and create a new eBook with Pages that includes the following sections from the Wikipedia entry for A. A. Milne (you don't have to include all of the Wikipedia information for each section): life, literary career, religious views, works, and references.

18. Export your e-book as an ePub document and use iTunes to sync it to your mobile device, then open it with iBooks and go through Steps 9 through 16 with your book (but search for a different word you know will appear in you book).

19. Go to the iBookstore on your iPad and download the sample chapters for A. O. Wilson's *Life on Earth*.

20. Practice going to a different part of the book using gestures, and opening and closing a page in each section. (Hint: tap, pinch gesture)

21. Go to Page 6 and practice opening and closing the embedded video.

22. Practice adding highlights, underlines, and notes, as well as looking up words and using Speak Selection to have the text read aloud as you did for Winnie the Pooh.

23. Rotate the iPad to the portrait orientation. What happened? Use the table of contents to return to the welcome chapter. (Hint: pinch in)

24. Rotate the iPad to landscape orientation and go to Page 8, and then tap on the word "molecules" to open its glossary entry. Tap on Glossary Index to see other terms in the glossary. Tap Done to return to the book.

25. Open the Study Cards for the book and select Chapter 14 on the left side of the screen (make sure you're in landscape orientation). Tap Study Cards on the right side and go through a few of the cards. (Hint: Flick) Practice flipping a few of the cards, then when you're done, tap Done a few times to return to the book.

26. Install iBooks Author (free) from the App Store on your computer and create a simple book using one of the included templates.

27. Add a review widget at the end of the first chapter and practice creating a simple multiple-choice quiz with three questions.

28. Preview the book on your iPad by connecting the iPad with a USB cable, opening the iBooks app, and choosing Preview in iBooks Author.

29. Go to the page where you added the review widget and practice taking your quiz.

30. Install the free Kindle app and open the included *Welcome to Kindle* book. Practice changing some of the text display options. (Hint: Tap on the screen and use the controls at the bottom of the screen.)

31. Install the free StoryKit app and create a short story of your favorite vacation. Use the drawing and recording features to illustrate the pages and record your own narration. (Optional: Install Book Creator or Creative Book Builder and create a short story with images and audio narration.)

32. Install the free iTunes U app and browse through the various collections until you find one that interests you. (Hint: Tap Catalog to browse available titles.). When you find a collection you like, subscribe to it and listen to/watch the first episode.

33. In the iTunes U app, find a course and subscribe to it. Download a book in that course and practice adding a note and viewing it back in the iTunes U app.

34. Optional: Purchase one of the iWork apps and go through the included Get Started tutorial to become more familiar with the app's features.

35. Optional: Purchase iMovie for the iPad and after reading through some of the help (Hint: tap the question mark in the lower-left corner after opening the app), create a short movie about your community by recording a video clip of an important landmark. Practice adding a title and importing a few photos from the Web. (Hint: Tap and hold any photo in the Safari app, then choose Save Image to add it to your Camera Roll, where it will be available to iMovie.) To complete your movie, add your own voiceover narration explaining some of the photos, and upload your movie to YouTube.

4

Communication and Social Supports

The combination of affordability, portability, ease of use, and social acceptability have made the iPad a popular option for parents and professionals who work with children with autism and related disabilities that affect communication and social interactions. Whereas similar communication devices might cost about $7,000, a kit consisting of an iPad, portable speakers, a protective case, and a communication app can all be purchased for around $1,000. This kit, paired with the iPad's claimed battery life of about ten hours, provides a portable solution that can last a typical school day for a child who relies on the device for communication. The portability also means the child can learn and play with the device anywhere, whether at home or at school. As for its ease of use, the iPad's touch screen interface invites children to do what comes naturally: touch. There is no physical keyboard or mouse (along with the concept of a separate cursor) for children to master before they can interact with the apps, as everything can be done with the touch of a finger on the screen. Add to that the fact that the iPad has become a popular and socially desirable gadget without the stigma of other assistive technologies, and it is easy to see why many parents and professionals choose the iPad for meeting the communication and social needs of children with autism and other related disabilities. The bigger screen of the iPad allows it to display more of the symbols used by many communication apps (and at a larger size) than a device with a smaller screen.

That is not to say the iPad and similar touch screen devices do not also have some drawbacks for use with children who have autism and related disabilities. One of these is the concern that children will become too focused (even obsessed) with an app at the expense of other learning opportunities. However, this concern can be addressed through the enforcement of firm boundaries with regard to screen time, such as by using timer apps to track how much time the child can spend using the device at a time. At the other extreme, some children may accidentally exit out of the apps they need for communication and then not know how to get back in. This issue was addressed in iOS 6 with a feature called Guided Access that allows for a single app mode for such a situation. Guided Access is discussed in more detail in Chapter 9, which focuses on how to manage the use of the iPad in the classroom.

Universal Design for Learning (UDL) Guidelines

- *Multiple and Flexible Means of Representation*: The apps for children with autism and related disabilities tend to have colorful graphics along with animation and sound cues. This multimodal approach can work well for many children with autism who are visual learners. Many of the apps available for the iPad focus on a single skill or learning task. Along with the wide selection of apps, this means parents can scaffold learning by starting with simpler apps and then moving to more sophisticated apps as the child is ready for them.
- *Multiple and Flexible Means of Expression*: The direct method of access through a touch screen on the iPad is easy to master for most children. For those with fine motor difficulties, a number of switch devices are now available to facilitate access. For executive functioning, the Guided Access feature can help children stay on task, and a number of apps are available for creating visual schedules and social stories that model appropriate behaviors.
- *Multiple and Flexible Means of Engagement*: On one hand, many of the apps for the iPad include voiceover narration and a simple interface to guide children as they learn how to use the app without the help of adults, and this promotes autonomy. On the other hand, the social acceptability of the device facilitates interactions between children with disabilities and their nondisabled peers, opening the door for collaboration during both

learning and play. Also, many apps are available to teach coping skills for dealing with a number of challenging social situations for children with disabilities such as autism (going to the doctor, the mall, or any new social situation that might cause anxiety).

The power of the iPad for students with autism and related disabilities comes from the large collection of apps that have been created to address communication and social challenges, a few of which I explore in more detail in this chapter. One of the apps that I have found valuable for sorting through the many apps for people with autism and related disabilities is Autism Apps by touch Autism. This app provides a comprehensive list of apps that are used with and by people with autism, arranged into more than 30 categories with searchable descriptions and reviews when they are available. You can download Autism Apps from http://bit.ly/AustismApps.

Communication Apps

Checkpoint 4.1—Vary the methods for response and navigation.
Checkpoint 4.2—Optimize access to tools and assistive technologies.
Checkpoint 5.1—Use multiple media for communication.
Checkpoint 5.2—Use multiple tools for construction and composition.

Some people either can't speak clearly, or at all. The cause of this speaking difficulty varies, and can be either physical or cognitive/social in nature. To communicate, those with these communication difficulties need to use tools that either augment their limited talking ability or help them communicate in an alternate way: alternative and augmentative communication or AAC. For the reasons I listed at the beginning of this chapter, the iPad has become a popular solution for those with AAC needs, and the number of apps focusing on communication has grown at a rapid pace. These apps range from those that include picture symbols the person taps on the screen to build a word or sentence to those that are text-based and include sophisticated word-prediction features. Some apps, such as Proloquo2Go combine both features into a complete solution that can address the needs of both young children as well as adults. Before I look at some of these apps, I want to mention some of the things I look for as I evaluate communication apps:

- *Support for customization*: For apps that rely on symbols, the app should, at a minimum, allow me to add my own symbols to customize it for the individual child who will use it (include items from their everyday life, etc.).

- *Ease of use*: The app should not present unnecessary barriers to communication because of its design (confusing interface, etc.).
- *High-quality voices* (or the ability to record human speech). Apps with high-quality voices tend to cost more because the voices have to be licensed from their developer. However, the high-quality voices also result in a more pleasing and easier to understand voice output from the apps that use them.
- *Support for accessibility features such as VoiceOver*: I have included this requirement because many of the new switch interfaces for the iPad rely on VoiceOver to provide access for switch users. Of course, the fact that support for VoiceOver can also accommodate the needs of students with multiple disabilities, including low vision, is an additional benefit.
- *Technical Support*: While the app should be intuitive and easy to use, help documents should also be easy to access if there is a problem, and it should be easy to contact the developer when a need to do so arises. I also look at how active the developer is in releasing updates to the app. This shows me how committed she or he is to improving the app for users.

Symbol and Scene-Based AAC Apps

While some of the apps in this section also include an onscreen keyboard (often with word prediction and other features that make typing easier), many of these apps are intended for young children. Thus, they rely on symbols or scene-based displays to provide communication options for those who are nonverbal or who have limited verbal communication skills.

- Proloquo2Go

$189.99

Proloquo2Go has long been one of the leading apps for AAC on the App Store. The app includes a library of more than 14,000 SymbolStix picture symbols, but the users can also import their photos to add additional symbols. As the user taps the symbols, which are arranged in a grid view, they are added to a message window to form a sentence that can be spoken aloud with a number of high-quality voices (including some children voices). Custom pronunciations can be added for hard to pronounce proper names, and the grid view can be customized by reordering buttons, changing the appearance of individual pages or buttons, and hiding or dimming buttons that are not being used. A separate typing view provides advanced word prediction and the ability to speak the words as the user types, and a Recents view tracks recently spoken phrases. With the 2.0 update, Proloquo2Go added support for multiple users to make it easier to use the app with multiple children in a school or clinical setting.

- SonoFlex

$99.99

SonoFlex includes more than 11,000 SymbolStix symbols that can be arranged into two different home page types. In the Common Vocabulary Home Page, core vocabulary is arranged in the center of the page with different context-specific fringe vocabularies accessible through buttons on the right side of the screen (more than 50 such contexts are available). The parent or teacher can also select an alternative home page style where only the contexts are shown. Communication takes place as follows: The child selects a core word, then a word from one of the category pages (e.g., verbs, people, places, etc.), followed by words from one of the context pages to complete the message, which is then spoken aloud by one of the five included Acapela voices. Symbols are color coded according to the Fitzgerald Key (with different colors for people, places, verbs, etc.), and the parent or teacher can customize each symbol by importing photos. Other features include an onscreen keyboard (in ABC order), a history option to recall previous messages, and a Quick Phrases feature for frequently used small talk.

- TouchChat

$149.99

TouchChat is an AAC app that includes more than 10,000 SymbolStix symbols, and parents and teachers can add their own symbols using the camera on their devices as well. The app has four included page sets (with additional page sets available as in-app purchases). One of the included page sets (spelling) has an onscreen keyboard with four-word prediction cells. Page sets typically consist of linked pages that include a number of programmable buttons. Tapping on each button adds the associated word or phrase to the message window, where the message can be spoken aloud by one of the seven

included voices (five U.S. English and two British English).
Buttons can also include recorded speech, or they can be programmed to include actions such as navigating to a different
page, playing an audio or video file stored on the device, or
clearing the display. A unique feature of this app is that the
phrase in the message window can be shared as an email or text
message, Facebook or Twitter update, or even uploaded to a
Tumblr blog. I love apps that include these social features
because they provide a valuable outlet for people with disabilities to remain engaged with family and friends even if they
live far away. Custom page sets, once created with the app, can
be shared through an iShare community.

- Tap Speak

  TapSpeak is actually a set of communication apps that range
  from the simple Tap Speak Button to the more complex Tap
  Speak Choice. Tap to Speak Button ($29.99) is a single-message
  cause and effect communication app. When the child taps a
  large button on the screen, he or she will hear a recorded message played back. A plus version of the app ($49.99) is also
  available that includes 4,500 PCS symbols that can be used for
  the buttons. Tap Speak Sequence for iPad builds on the functionality of Tap Speak Button by allowing a parent or teacher to
  create message sequences consisting of several picture symbols, each of which can have its own voice recording. Like Tap
  Speak Button, the app is available in a standard version ($29.99)
  that only supports geometric shapes and the user's images, or
  a plus version ($49.99) that includes 4,500 PCS symbols (these
  symbols are also available as an in-app purchase if you buy the
  standard version first). At the high end, Tap Speak Choice for
  iPad ($149.99) can be used to build single or multilevel com-
  munication boards. Each board can have from 1 to 56 cells, and
  each cell can contain a symbol with either text to speech or a
  voice recording. The Tap Speak iPad apps all have support for
  switch interfaces from RJ Cooper and AbleNet, or you can use
  the iPad screen as a switch. Tap Speak Choice supports one and
  two switch scanning as well.

- SoundingBoard

  Free

  SoundingBoard can be used to create custom communication
  boards. Each board can have from one to nine cells, and each cell

can include either an AbleNet symbol from the included library or a photo from the user's camera. When a cell is selected, it plays a voice recording, and cells can also be linked to other boards to create a multilevel communication system. The app includes a small number of situation-specific communication boards (yes/no, shopping, money, etc.), and a few additional boards are available from AbleNet as in-app purchases. Sounding Board supports one and two switch access with visual and auditory scanning (a short recorded prompt is played when the cell has focus, a great feature for using the switch access with a student who also has a visual impairment). Supported switches include RJ Cooper's switch interface and AbleNet's Blue 2 switch interface. The app can collect some usage data, such as information about the most popular boards or symbols, and this information can be emailed as a CSV file from the app.

- Scene and Heard

  $49.99

  Scene and Heard is an app for constructing visual scene displays (VSDs) intended for beginning communicators or those who have significant cognitive and linguistic difficulties. Each VSD consists of an image with hotspots that can play a recorded sound, pull up a symbol or a group of symbols, launch a video, or link to another scene. In addition to a few premade scenes, you can build your own using the more than 12,000 included Widget symbols or your own photos. The app supports one and two switch access with visual scanning (with switch interfaces from RJ Cooper or Therapy Box).

To download the symbol and scene-based communication apps mentioned in this section, visit http://pinterest.com/mlearning4all/aac-symbol/.

Text-Based AAC Apps

The apps in this section are intended primarily for literate users who have conditions such as apraxia, ALS, stroke, traumatic brain injury, cerebral palsy, Parkinson's, or muscular dystrophy.

- Verbally and Verbally+

  Free and $99

  Verbally is a text-to-speech app with word prediction. Some core words and frequently spoken phrases are provided with both versions, but the phrases can only be edited with the premium version. The premium version also adds higher-quality Acapela voices, a conversation history for recalling previously spoken phrases, and the ability to organize phrases using folders. The text to speech can be set to speak each word as the user types it, and the keyboard includes a button for playing a sound to get the other person's attention.

- Predictable

  $159.99

  Predictable is a text-to-speech and word prediction app that has support for one and two switch access with visual scanning (using switch interfaces from Therapy Box or RJ Cooper). A touch-anywhere feature also allows the entire screen to be used as a switch with a scanning mode. In addition to the onscreen keyboard, the app also has support for handwriting input. As with similar apps, Predictable includes the option to save frequently used phrases and to organize them into categories that can include images (either included clipart or your own images). A nice feature of this app is the ability to share the messages in email messages or as Tweets or Facebook status updates.

- Speak It!

  $1.99

  This simple and inexpensive text-to-speech app includes word highlighting. In addition to the included U.S. and British English male and female voices, a few additional voices in other languages are available as in-app purchases. Spoken phrases can be saved for later use or converted into audio files that can be emailed to someone else.

Apps for Language Development

Checkpoint 5.3—Build fluencies with graduated levels of support for practice and performance.

A number of apps have been developed by speech language pathologists to help children who have difficulties with articulation or speech sound production. While parents can use these apps at home to improve a child's communication, their true power is realized when used by a trained professional such as an SLP within a clinical setting. The iPad, in combination with articulation apps, can replace the boxes of picture cards SLPs have traditionally relied on for articulation practice. Many of the apps in this section also allow for data collection so educators can set appropriate goals for each child and track progress in language development.

- Articulate It!

  $38.99

  This app includes more than 1,200 images with all the phonemes of the English language. The app can be used with multiple students, and students can have their own goals for phonemes, phonological processes, and manner of articulation. The app tracks progress for each student during a session, and results can be printed (with an AirPrint compatible printer) or emailed. For independent practice, the child can tap on each image to hear a recording of the word, and then use the built-in recording feature to practice saying it for comparison. These recordings are saved along with the other data collected by the app, and they can be included as an attachment when emailing the results.

- ArtikPix

  Free (lite), $29.99 (full)

  This app is available in both a free lite version and a full paid version. The full version includes 21 card decks, with 40 cards for each phoneme (913 total cards). The free version only includes one deck with "th" cards, but additional decks are available as in-app purchases. For the flashcard activity, the SLP or teacher selects the sound and sound group (beginning th, middle th, etc.) for the student to practice. During the activity, a group scoring feature can be used to collect data on up to four students. Students can hear the word on the card as well as use a built-in recording feature to hear themselves say it. The matching activity provides a fun way for children to practice their speech sounds while data are still collected. In this mode, words can be randomized in easy (3 pairs), medium (6 pairs), or hard (10 pairs) levels. The app automatically converts the tallies recorded during the activities to percentages, and results can be shared via email, saved to a Google Spreadsheet, or copied to the clipboard (in case you want to paste it into a word processing app).

- PhonoPix

  $24.99

  PhonoPix is meant to be a companion to ArtikPix. It includes 10 decks with 40 minimal pairs in each deck (400 total pairs). These minimal pairs contrast children's incorrect responses with the target responses. As with ArtikPix, the flashcard activity allows children to practice by listening to the recorded audio in each card first, then recording their own voice for comparison. With Version 2.0, the app added group scoring for up to four children.

- Spanish Artik

  $19.99

  Spanish Artik is an app for helping Spanish-speaking children practice their sounds. This app includes more than 450 images and many of the features of the other apps in this section (recording students' voices for comparison, data collection, etc.).

- VAST Autism 1–Core

  $4.99

  VAST Autism 1–Core is one of a series of apps from SpeakinMotion that focus on providing video modeling for speech. The apps are intended for students with autism and apraxia. Each app includes a series of videos organized into a hierarchy beginning with syllables and ending in complete sentences. Each video includes the written word or phrase, and a mirroring feature works with the forward facing camera on iOS devices to provide visual feedback to the person using the app as she or he practices saying the word or phrase in the video.

To download the apps for language development mentioned in this section, visit http://pinterest.com/mlearning4all/speech/.

Sign Language Apps

Checkpoint 1.2—Offer alternatives for auditory information.
Checkpoint 2.1—Clarify vocabulary and symbols.

Checkpoint 2.4—Promote understanding across languages.
Checkpoint 2.5—Illustrate through multiple media.

A number of apps are available for learning sign language on the iPad. Some of these apps even have a translation feature to facilitate communication with someone who is deaf.

- Sign4Me

  $12.99

  This is the only app I know that presents sign language in 3D. It is also a Signed English translator. With Sign4Me, you type the word or phrase into a text box at the top of the screen, and when you press Done, a character (an avatar) signs them on the screen. You can use your finger to move around the character and see the signs from different angles, and even use a pinch gesture to zoom in for a closer look. Tapping once on the screen reveals controls for adjusting the speed of the signing or turning off the looping feature. The sign library for Sign4Me contains more than 11,500 words that can be typed in sentences, phrases, individually, or in alphabet form. Typing in "ABCDE" without any spaces will go through the signs for the alphabet.

- ASL Dictionary

  $3.99

  ASL video dictionary with more than 4,800 signed words and common phrases, including more than 55 idioms. A professional sign language interpreter signs each word or phrase in a short video. Each video can be looped, slowed down, and marked as a favorite. The app does not require Internet access, which is a big plus for use in schools with limited Internet connectivity.

- Signing Time ASL Dictionary Flash Cards

  $2.99

  This app for early childhood includes 145 flashcards. Each flashcard includes a video with sound, and the app includes a quiz feature to let children test their knowledge of the ASL words.

The sign language apps mentioned in this section can be downloaded by visiting http://pinterest.com/mlearning4all/sign-language/.

Social Skills Apps

In addition to communication difficulties, children with autism often have difficulties with social interactions. The apps in this section can be helpful for addressing some of the learning difficulties many children with autism and related disabilities have that affect their social functioning. This includes difficulties with attention, task and event sequencing, organization and planning, time concepts, and making transitions. To address these difficulties, a number of apps incorporate high-quality graphics into visual schedules that help children with autism successfully complete tasks. Video modeling and social story apps can help these children learn appropriate behaviors for a variety of settings. Along with these supports, the social acceptability of the iPad itself can open a whole new world of social interaction for children with autism by providing them with a device that invites communication and interaction from their peers.

Visual Schedule Apps

Checkpoint 6.2—Support planning and strategy development.
Checkpoint 6.4—Enhance capacity to monitor progress.
Checkpoint 7.1—Optimize individual choice and autonomy.
Checkpoint 7.3—Minimize threats and distractions.

Visual schedule apps can be used to provide students with a structure for their daily activities. These apps can reduce anxiety during transitions by allowing students to anticipate what is going to happen next. They are also helpful when teaching any task that involves a series of steps. Within the structure of visual schedules, students can begin to do some choice making when they start to provide input into the order of activities. Along with visual schedules, a number of reward chart apps can be used to help reinforce positive behaviors, and timer apps provide a visual way to help children improve their time on task.

- iCommunicate

  $49.99

  iCommunicate is an app for designing visual schedules, but it can also be used to create communication and choice boards, flashcards, and more. When designing a visual schedule with this app, you can use any of the included 10,000 SymbolStix symbols, take your own photo with the iPad's built-in cameras, or do an online search for images. Each storyboard can be up to 4 images across and 10 down. The app includes high-quality iSpeech voices for text to speech, but only when an Internet connection is available. At other times, a lower-quality open source voice from OpenEars is used. You can also record your voice for either each symbol or the entire storyboard. Each schedule is completed by flicking with one finger to navigate to the next task. A tap and hold with one finger will indicate the task has been completed successfully (green checkmark), while a tap and hold with two fingers will indicate that it has not (red circle with a line through it). You can also enable a Move to Next feature in the settings to automatically advance to the next task on a successful try. Storyboards can be emailed or printed to a compatible printer.

- Chore Pad HD

  $4.99

  ChorePad HD is a weekly chore chart for the iPad with support for multiple children. Children can see their chores in a weekly view, or rotate the iPad to see just the chores for the current day. To set up the chore chart, chores are first added to a chore chest, and then assigned to individual children as needed. Each chore can be set up to occur only on specific days, or to repeat at a set interval (every week).

- iReward

  $4.99

  iReward can be used to set up a reward schedule that reinforces positive behaviors using a visual reward. When a task is completed, the child can receive auditory feedback from a recording of your voice, and each reward can also include two images if you want to set it up as an if-then reward. The iReward app supports reward schedules for multiple children.

- Time Timer

  $2.99

  Time Timer is a simple visual timer consisting of a colored disk that gets smaller as the time elapses. The app has three timer modes: In the original mode, the disc represents 60 minutes, in the custom mode, it represents any amount of time (hours, minutes, and seconds), and in clock mode, it shows the elapsed time along with a clock face. The latest version of this app allows for timers to be saved so that they can be reused without going through all the setup steps, and up to four timers can be set and shown at the same time. If you have a second device (such as an iPod touch), you can use Time Timer to limit the amount of screen time a child has.

To download the scheduling apps mentioned in this section, visit http://pinterest.com/mlearning4all/visual-schedules/.

Modeling Apps

Checkpoint 9.2—Facilitate coping skills and strategies.

The apps in this section are divided into two groups: those that include premade social stories for modeling appropriate behaviors, and those that allow the parent or teacher to create the story based on the specific needs of the child. Both types of apps have their place for modeling work. The apps with the premade stories can save time by already including high-quality images and voice recordings. The ones with the ability to create new stories allow the parent or teacher to include photos from the child's actual home or school environment, making the stories more meaningful for the child.

- Model Me Going Places 2

  Free

  Model Me Going Places 2 is a visual teaching tool for helping children navigate challenging settings in the community. The app is based on the Model Me Going Places DVD series. Each of the six included locations has a slideshow of children modeling appropriate behavior. These slideshows include a voice recording of a child's voice, which reads the text at the bottom of the screen. Navigation is simple: Tap the button in the lower-right corner to go to the next slide, or the button on the lower-left corner to go back. There is also a slideshow button for automatically advancing the pages/screens.

- Hidden Curriculum

  $1.99

  Two Hidden Curriculum apps are available: one for children and one for teens and adults. The goal of these apps is to serve as conversation starters for discussing unwritten social rules that we encounter every day that may cause confusion to students with autism spectrum disorder and other related disabilities.

- Stories2Learn

  $13.99

  Stories2Learn is preloaded with six social stories that can be used to teach social skills in the areas of reciprocal play, nonverbal communication, playground and school rules, and turn taking. In addition to the preloaded stories, you can create new stories with your photos, text, and audio messages.

- Pictello

  $18.99

  Pictello creates digital storybooks that can be used as social stories for modeling appropriate behaviors. Each page in a Pictello book can include an image with text, and the text can be read aloud by the built-in text to speech or you can record yourself reading it. The app includes a wizard to guide the user through the creation of a book.

- SonicPics

  $2.99

  Although not intended as a social story app, SonicPics includes all the tools needed to create a simple social story with high-quality images and voice narration. With this slideshow app, you take a few photos with your device and record a narration track. As you narrate the slideshow, you can flick with one finger to advance the slides, and the audio will be synchronized with the images.

For a more fun take on social stories, you can use a number of puppet show and comic book creation apps. My favorites for puppet shows are Sock Puppets, Toontastic, and Puppet Pals. These apps are free, but also include in-app purchases for additional props to use in the puppet shows. The general idea with these apps is that you create a character (a puppet), and as you move that character around on the stage, you can record audio narration. For comic books, my favorite app is Comic Life ($4.99). The app includes nine templates to help you get started with authoring comics that can include images taken with your device's camera, thought bubbles, and free-floating text.

To download the modeling apps in this section, visit http://pinterest.com/mlearning4all/modeling/.

Apps for Learning About Emotions

Checkpoint 9.2—Facilitate personal coping skills and strategies.

Many children with autism have a difficult time with eye gaze, as well as with picking up social cues and accurately reading others' emotional states. The apps in this section provide practice with reading different emotional states, as this is an important skill that helps with developing peer relationships.

- Look In My Eyes

  $2.99 each

  Look In My Eyes is a series of apps that use game play to help children develop their eye gaze. With each game, the child looks into a photo of another child with numbers in the eyes. After a few seconds, the child is asked to indicate what numbers were in the photo. After four correct tries, the child is able to get a reward to build a virtual world (restaurant, mechanic shop, or undersea world depending on the app).

- AutismXpress

  Free

  AutismXpress includes a number of emotions (happy, sad, surprised) and bodily states (hungry, sleepy, sickly). For each emotion, tapping the icon will launch a full screen clip with an animation showing the emotion and a matching sound effect. The app is free, but also available is a paid AutismXpress Pro app that includes two games: one that asks children to match the emotions and one that gives them the name of an emotion and asks them to select the matching icon for it.

- The Grouchies

  Free

  The Grouchies is a free book app that uses rhymes to show children ways they can turn around grouchy moods. The goal of the app is also to show children how their moods can affect their family and friends.

To download the apps in this section, visit http://pinterest.com/ mlearning4all/emotions/.

Sensory Stimulus Control Apps

Checkpoint 7.3—Minimize threats and distractions.
Checkpoint 9.2—Facilitate coping skills and strategies.

While not limited to children with autism, the meltdown is a common event for many children with special needs. One strategy for dealing with such meltdowns is to find a way to refocus or calm the child. A number of apps are available for iOS devices that can be used for this purpose.

- Pocket Pond

  Free

  Pocket Pond is a virtual pond with soothing nature sounds. Touching the screen creates a ripple in the water with a matching sound effect. One thing to note is that this app includes in-app purchases for additional ponds and creatures (crabs, frogs, etc.). These in-app purchases can be disabled using the Restrictions feature of iOS (Settings > General > Restrictions). The app also has a thunderstorm effect that you can turn off by swiping up from the lower-right corner and tapping a few times next to Thunderstorm.

- Bloom

  $3.99

  Bloom is not only a great calming app, but also a way to allow children to express their creativity through music. With Bloom, each tap of the screen creates a new note indicated by a colored circle, or you can just let the app play on its own. Tapping the Settings button in the lower-right corner of the screen allows you to change the mood and set a sleep timer if you want to use the app to help with sleep problems. The same developers (musicians Brian Eno and Peter Chilvers) have created another app called Trope that allows you to create soundscapes by tracing abstract shapes on the screen, varying the tone with each movement.

- Splatter

  Free

  Splatter is a great app for children with autism who enjoy painting with vibrant colors and tactile learning. Drawings are created by tapping and dragging anywhere on the screen. A fast drag results in a thin line, a slow one in a thick one. The color can be changed by tapping on the color strip at the bottom of the screen, and the drawing on the screen can be saved to the Camera Roll by tapping the button on the right side of the strip. One issue with this app is that clearing the screen requires a shaking motion, and not all children are able to perform this action. Unfortunately, this shaking motion cannot be simulated with the AssistiveTouch feature built into iOS. This means a parent will need to help if the child wants to clear the screen to start a new drawing.

To download the sensory apps in this section, visit http://pinterest .com/mlearning4all/sensory/.

Data Collection

A number of data collection apps are available to allow parents, teachers, and therapists to collect information about a child's behaviors to get a better idea of why they occur. The app that I have found the most useful for this purpose is Behavior Tracker Pro ($29.99). This app can be used to collect four types of data: frequency and duration, ABC, high-frequency behavior, and interval.

Figure 4.1   Main Screen for Behavior Tracker Pro

For each type of data collection, you begin by indicating clients (the child or children to be observed) and an observer. The steps for actually recording the information will depend on the type of data. For frequency and duration data, double-tap on the green area to begin recording, and then double-tap on the red area to stop it.

Figure 4.2   Screen for Collecting Frequency and Duration Data in Behavior Tracker Pro

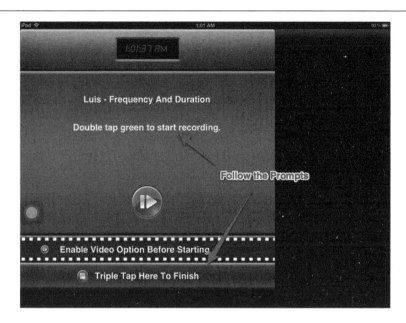

When you're done recording, you will see a list open on the right where you can choose the observed behavior.

Figure 4.3   Behaviors That Can Be Selected From List on Right Side of Behavior Tracker Pro Interface

Tapping done will close the list and allow you to start recording the next behavior. To end the session, triple-tap the blue area near the bottom of the screen. The steps for recording ABC data are similar, but instead of selecting just a behavior from the list, you will also select an antecedent (wants something) and a consequence (blocked access to reinforce). Behavior Tracker Pro can generate graphs of the recorded data right on the device, or you can export the data via email into CSV and XML formats that can be imported into Microsoft Excel if you prefer to use that program to create your charts. You can also use your device's camera to record video along with the behavior data. While a tutorial is not available within the app, you can choose Settings, Help, and Documentation to access a user's guide and an overview video on the developer's Web site at www.behaviortrackerpro.com.

5

VoiceOver and Supports for Low Vision

Braille and large print have been the traditional means of accessing information for people with visual disabilities, but braille and large print materials take time to produce and do not have the flexibility of digital content. Using the accessibility features of the iPad, such as the VoiceOver screen reader, Zoom, and Invert Colors, students with visual disabilities can access the same information that is available to their nondisabled peers without the need to wait for a special version to be published just for them. Along with a number of third-party apps, these features can be used to provide accommodations for students who have visual disabilities ranging from low vision to the complete loss of their eyesight.

VoiceOver:
Universal Design for Learning (UDL) Guidelines

- *Multiple and Flexible Means of Representation:* Before a student can learn from the information presented, that student must first be able to perceive it. By using text to speech to convert the information in textbooks and other print educational materials into a format that is more accessible for people with visual disabilities, screen readers such as VoiceOver reduce the barriers to learning by ensuring that information is perceptible to all learners. As long as the author creates the content in a way that follows a few accessibility best practices, students with visual disabilities can use VoiceOver to have the information in educational materials read aloud to them or output as braille on a refreshable braille display. For students with low vision, iOS includes Zoom and Invert Colors to allow them to customize the display to match their level of remaining vision.

- *Multiple and Flexible Means of Expression:* VoiceOver supports a number of ways for students to express what they know in writing: They can type the information using the onscreen keyboard or a physical keyboard connected through Bluetooth or dictate the information on devices that support the Dictation and Siri features. VoiceOver is also compatible with a number of recording apps students with visual disabilities can use to provide their responses in audio form.

- *Multiple and Flexible Means of Engagement:* While VoiceOver includes a high-quality voice, it still does not sound as natural as a human voice. However, through a number of accessible podcasting, reading services, and audiobook apps, students with visual disabilities can access content that has been recorded by human beings. A number of podcasts have been created by other people with visual disabilities and provide advice on topics of interest to those who are blind or have low vision (adjusting to having a guide dog, using a white cane for navigation, seeking employment, etc.). Through accessible social media apps, students with visual disabilities can not only stay engaged with topics in the news that interest them, but also build strong peer relationships around these topics with like-minded people.

Checkpoint 1.3—Offer alternatives for visual information.

VoiceOver is the built-in screen reader for iOS devices, such as the iPad, that describes what appears onscreen aloud to people who have visual disabilities. Using VoiceOver, students with visual disabilities that prevent them from reading a traditional textbook can instead have the content in a digital version of the textbook read aloud to them by the screen reader. Most textbook publishers now provide digital versions of their textbooks that can be accessed by someone with a visual disability in this way. With the release of iBooks 2 for the iPad, Apple partnered with some of the major textbooks publishers to make a new kind of digital textbook, known as an iBook, available on the iBookstore. These textbooks are compatible with VoiceOver and the other accessibility features available on the iPad. As the number of textbook titles available in the iBookstore grows, this has the potential to provide even more access to textbooks for students with visual disabilities. Furthermore, using the free iBooks Author app for the Mac, teachers can create their own accessible materials that students can access on mobile devices. For example, a teacher could use iBooks Author to provide worksheets, review questions, and other materials in an accessible format.

VoiceOver is also a powerful tool for allowing students with visual disabilities to access content on the Web. This is important because many teachers are increasingly relying on online content to supplement the textbook. For example, a teacher might assign a project to a social studies class asking students to research a current event on the Web. Students with visual disabilities can do the same kind of online research as the rest of the class by using VoiceOver to access Web sites with the Safari app on a mobile device. After finishing the research, these students can use a note-taking app to complete the written part of the assignment, which can then be emailed to the teacher from the iPad using the Mail app.

All of Apple's built-in apps on the iPad have been designed to work with VoiceOver, and many third-party apps now include support for the feature. VoiceOver can be customized to match each student's preferred reading rate, and it supports more than 30 languages and dialects for students with visual disabilities that speak a language other than English. VoiceOver is also compatible with more than 30 Bluetooth wireless braille displays. These displays allow someone with a visual impairment to read VoiceOver output in braille, and some displays even include keys that can be used to control the mobile device while VoiceOver is turned on. The braille support allows students to choose the format that works best for them. Students who are proficient in braille can choose to access information in that format.

Getting Started With VoiceOver

The key to using VoiceOver is the VoiceOver cursor. This is a black rectangle that represents the currently selected item on the screen, which is what VoiceOver will read aloud.

Figure 5.1   VoiceOver Cursor

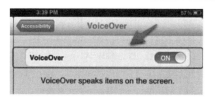

By following the VoiceOver cursor, a sighted person can keep track of what someone with a visual impairment is doing on his or her iPad. The VoiceOver cursor encourages collaboration between students with visual disabilities and their sighted peers. Students can work side by side, and even if the student with the disability is using headphones to listen to VoiceOver, the other student can keep up by tracking the VoiceOver cursor.

To move the VoiceOver cursor and change what VoiceOver reads aloud, you can just touch a different part of the screen with one finger. VoiceOver will even read the items at the top of the screen, including the time, the Wi-Fi signal strength, and the battery status. Another way to navigate your iPad with VoiceOver is by using a set of special gestures. For example, to move to the next item, you would use one finger to flick to the right, and to move to the previous item, you would use one finger to flick to the left. Once you hear the desired item announced, you have to double-tap anywhere on the screen to open it (if it is an app) or to perform the desired action (if it is a button or other interface element). This double-tap is required to prevent people who are blind from accidentally opening apps or tapping the wrong button. For a full list of the gestures supported by VoiceOver, please see Appendix B. To view a video showing how basic navigation with VoiceOver on the iPad works, scan QR Code 5.1 or visit http://bit.ly/VoiceOverNavigation.

QR Code 5.1
Basic
Navigation
Techniques
With
VoiceOver

VoiceOver includes a practice feature to help someone who is sighted and who works with students with visual disabilities learn the supported gestures. To practice the various VoiceOver gestures do the following:

1. Choose General > Accessibility > VoiceOver in Settings.

Figure 5.2   VoiceOver Option in the Accessibility Pane of Settings

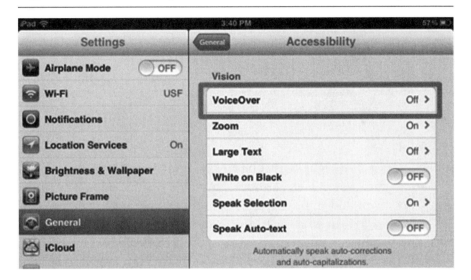

2. Tap the On/Off switch to turn on VoiceOver.

Figure 5.3   Switch for Turning VoiceOver On

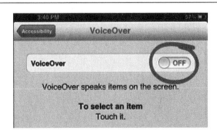

3. Select VoiceOver Practice (move your finger over the screen until VoiceOver announces that option) and double-tap with one finger.

Figure 5.4   VoiceOver Practice Button (Visible Only When VoiceOver Is On)

4. Flick to the right with one finger until VoiceOver announces, "Practice VoiceOver Gestures." At that point, you can perform one, two, and three finger taps, and gestures, such as flicks and swipes, to hear what each gesture does. You will also see a description of the gesture at the bottom of the screen after you perform it.
5. When you're finished, select Done by moving your finger to the top of the screen and double-tap with one finger.

Figure 5.5   VoiceOver Practice Screen

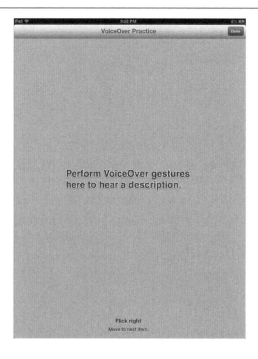

6. To turn off VoiceOver, select the VoiceOver toggle and double-tap with one finger.

One way to preserve the battery while using Voiceover is to dim the screen whenever possible, especially if the student does not have any functional vision that would make seeing the display necessary. Another solution is to buy an external battery that can be attached to the bottom of the device. Companies such as Mophie (www.mophie .com) sell such batteries as either a stand-alone attachment or as a case that includes the battery with it.

The Item Chooser

The item chooser was introduced in iOS 5 to provide another option for quickly navigating content. To activate the item chooser, perform a two-finger triple-tap. The item chooser will provide an alphabetic list of the items that can be selected on the current page or screen. These items can then be selected by flicking left or right with one finger. The item chooser also features a search field for searching within the current page or screen. To perform a search, select the search text box and double-tap with one finger. This will bring up the onscreen keyboard so that you can enter your search term using one of the typing modes discussed later in this chapter in the section on entering text (on some devices you can also select the Dictation button on the keyboard to speak the search term). To close the item chooser, perform a scrub gesture as follows: place two fingers on the screen and move them from side to side as if to form the letter "Z."

Reading With iBooks

The free iBooks e-reader app from Apple is compatible with VoiceOver. Students with visual disabilities can use this app to read PDF documents (if they contain text), ePub books, and iBooks interactive textbooks. The following VoiceOver gestures are supported in iBooks:

- Two-finger tap: stop speaking the current item. Tapping again with two fingers will resume speaking.
- Two-finger flick up: Read all from the top of the screen.

- Two-finger flick down: Read all from the current position. iBooks will even flip the pages while reading automatically.

Not all content in ePub and iBooks books is accessible with VoiceOver. For images to be accessible with VoiceOver, the author needs to include accessibility descriptions that will allow VoiceOver to describe the images to the reader. Unfortunately, with ePub books, the Pages authoring software does not have an option for adding an accessibility description for images. This means VoiceOver cannot properly describe the images in an ePub document created with Pages to a person who is blind. For iBooks textbooks, on the other hand, the iBooks Author software does have an option for adding an accessibility description for each image. For this reason, I recommend selecting the iBooks format for accessibility if you are authoring a book with images.

ePub is still an acceptable format for text-only documents because that format was developed with text in mind. Choosing ePub for text documents will also allow readers with low vision to take advantage of the many options for displaying text for ePub books in the iBooks app (text size, fonts, backgrounds, and night mode). As a bonus, ePub books can be accessed on a number of different devices and apps, whereas iBooks is an Apple format only supported by the iBooks app on the iPad. In the next section, I discuss the steps for adding accessibility descriptions in iBooks Author to ensure images are accessible with VoiceOver when the book is opened on the iPad.

Accessibility Descriptions

Checkpoint 1.3—Offer alternatives for visual information.

If you leave out the accessibility description for an image, VoiceOver may read the image's file name. This may confuse someone listening to the content with the VoiceOver screen reader. To prevent this from happening, add an accessibility description for each image as follows:

1. In iBooks Author, select the image that will be described and open the Inspector (View > Show Inspector).
2. Choose the Widget Inspector, then the Layout tab.
3. At the bottom of the Layout tab, enter the desired text in the Accessibility Description text box.

Figure 5.6 Accessibility Description Field in Layout Tab of Widget Inspector

Writing descriptions (or alternative text, as it is more commonly known in the accessibility world) is as much an art as it is a science, and much of it is subjective. Many sites provide information on how to write good alternative text for images on Web sites, but I have found little guidance on how to write descriptions for other online content, such as e-books. My recommendation would be to focus on three Cs when writing descriptions for images in iBooks Author:

- *Content:* As much as possible, accessibility descriptions should focus on the content of each image rather than its visual appearance. Thus, in a chemistry book that has an image of a scientist working in a lab, I would need to know that the scientist is placing test tubes in a centrifuge, but not that he or she is wearing a white lab coat, has short brown hair, and so on. There could be a few exceptions where you might need to focus on the visual details of the image, but these cases should be the exception rather than the rule.
- *Context:* The context in which the image is used is also important. For example, if I am writing a book on the Civil War and the text surrounding an image already explains a great deal about a famous general, I would try as much as possible to avoid redundancy in the accessibility description. I would ask

myself if the image of the general is already properly described in the surrounding text. If it is, then it might be more appropriate to mark it up as a decorative image (background). You could also reference the image in the surrounding text. In that case, in the text you would write, "See Figure X, or as seen on Figure X," and the matching accessibility description would be "Figure X." Avoiding redundancy also applies to the use of words such as "image" or "graphic" in the description. Since VoiceOver will announce that information when it comes across an image on the page (it will say, "Image" after reading the description), including these words in the descriptions makes them redundant.

- *Conciseness:* The final consideration is to keep the description as brief and concise as possible. I would try to keep it to no more than 8 to 10 words if possible. This will keep the accessibility description from disrupting the reader too much from the rest of the content.

Decorative images, such as dividers, are a special case. For those images, I would just enter the word "background" for the accessibility

QR Code 5.2
Accessibility
Descriptions

description. This will indicate to the reader that the image is not important for understanding the content, and the word is short enough that it should be easy to ignore. Leaving out the description may cause VoiceOver to read the entire file name, which is often not descriptive enough to avoid confusion. To learn more about accessibility descriptions, scan QR Code 5.2 or visit http://bit.ly/iBooksAuthorImages.

VoiceOver Configuration

The settings for VoiceOver can be found under General > Accessibility > VoiceOver in Settings. Some of these settings include the following:

- *Speak Hints:* When this option is turned on, VoiceOver will speak a hint when you select an item or control. For example, on the Home screen, VoiceOver will say, "Double-tap to open," after it announces the name of each item or folder. This feature will be helpful if you are new to VoiceOver, but as you become more proficient, you may not need the hints and can turn them off to save time.

- *Speaking Rate:* Use the slider to adjust the rate at which VoiceOver will read back information on the screen. Many people with disabilities have honed their ability to listen to content at very high speeds, and this setting allows them to adjust the VoiceOver speaking rate to match their listening needs. When working with a sighted teacher or peer, a student with a visual disability can use this slider to adjust the speaking rate so that it is more understandable to the other person.

- *Typing Feedback:* This is the feedback you will hear when you type. You can set VoiceOver to speak characters, words, both, or nothing, and there are separate options for the onscreen keyboard and for a physical keyboard such as an Apple wireless keyboard. I set this option to characters and words when using the onscreen keyboard and to only words when using an Apple wireless keyboard connected to my iPad. I have found that getting feedback as I type each character improves my accuracy with the onscreen keyboard, and hearing the whole word can help me catch spelling mistakes as I type. On the Apple Wireless keyboard, I know the keyboard layout well and can be more sure that I have selected the correct character, but I still have this option set to words to help me catch spelling mistakes as I type.

- *Use Pitch Change:* VoiceOver will raise the pitch when you enter a letter, and lower the pitch when you delete a letter. This feature provides an extra cue to help a student know whether the character she or he just heard has been entered or deleted. The additional feedback can be helpful when editing text for written assignments, and I generally leave this setting turned on. VoiceOver will also use a higher pitch when speaking the first item in a group (such as a list or table) and a lower pitch when it reaches the last item in the group. Again, this is additional feedback that can help a student who is unable to see understand how information is organized.

- *Use Compact Voice:* In iOS 5, an updated voice that is of a higher quality than the one available in previous versions of iOS was introduced. However, if you experience problems with the higher-quality voice on an older device, you can enable the compact voice instead.

- *Braille:* These options will control how a braille display interacts with VoiceOver, including the option to use contracted or eight-dot braille, or to change the location of the status cell. The status cell provides additional system information to the person using the braille display, such as indicating when the battery is running low and the device has to be charged. Paying attention to this status information will ensure the student's iPad does not run out of battery when she or he needs it most.

- *Rotor:* The rotor is a special gesture that consists of rotating two fingers on the device's screen, as if you are turning a virtual dial. The rotor is a shortcut that provides access to many VoiceOver settings without the need to go back into the Settings app, and I discuss this feature in more detail in its own section later in this chapter. The rotor setting will allow you to choose which items will be available when you use the rotor (such as a list of a Web page's headings, links, images, and so on).
- *Language Rotor:* The language rotor was introduced in iOS 4 and allows you to change the language used by VoiceOver at any time with the rotor gesture. In the VoiceOver settings, you can choose which languages will be available when you use the rotor to change the language. VoiceOver supports more than 30 languages and dialects, and additional languages are often added with each major update of the operating system. The support for multiple languages was intended to support the needs of students with visual disabilities who speak a language other than English. While the text to speech provided by VoiceOver could be helpful to other students, such as those who are learning English as their second language or struggling readers, I would instead recommend the Speak Selection feature discussed in the section on low vision for those students. That feature has less of a learning curve than VoiceOver while providing the same benefit (it actually uses the VoiceOver voice).

The Rotor

The rotor gesture is a special gesture that can be used to quickly change how VoiceOver is set up without going into the Settings. The rotor consists of two gestures:

1. Rotate two fingers on the screen to "turn" an invisible dial and choose from the available settings.
2. Flick up or down to select the next/previous option for each setting (such as going to the next heading, link, or form element on a Web page, or choosing a different speech rate or language).

The rotor provides quick access to many of the VoiceOver settings so that students can change these settings without having to close the app they're already in. VoiceOver settings that can be controlled with the rotor include the speech rate, the volume (which can be controlled separately from the main device volume), and the language. For example, a student reading a Web page who needs to change the speaking rate doesn't have to exit the Safari app and then go into the Settings. With the rotor, the student can quickly change the speaking rate and go right back to reading the content on the Web page. To view a brief video explaining how to adjust the speaking rate and language using the rotor, scan QR Code 5.3 or visit http://bit.ly/VoiceOverRotor.

QR Code 5.3
Using the Rotor to Adjust the VoiceOver Language and Speaking Rate

The rotor provides three different ways to hear text: by character, word, or line. Once you have selected one of these rotor settings, you can flick down to go to the next character, word, or line, or flick up will take you to the previous character, word, or line. I will usually set this option to words while I am editing to make it easier to select and delete individual words, then when I am done editing I will set it back to lines so that I can quickly review what I have written by moving through the text one line at a time.

The rotor used to be called the Web Rotor in previous versions of VoiceOver because of the many options it has for navigating Web content in the Safari app. For example, when browsing a Web page in the Safari app, you will find rotor options for navigating the page by headings, links, form controls, and many other page elements. A complete list of the options for Web navigation that can be added to the rotor is found in the Settings under Accessibility > VoiceOver > Rotor. For students with visual disabilities, these options can improve their ability to navigate Web pages more efficiently. Rather than reading the entire contents of the page, students can use the section headings to navigate to the section that has the content they need. Once they're in the right section, they can use other VoiceOver gestures to listen to the content in that section more carefully. To view a video showing how to navigate a Web page with the rotor, scan QR Code 5.4 or visit http://bit.ly/VoiceOverWebRotor.

QR Code 5.4
Using the Rotor for Navigation With VoiceOver

Custom Labels

Sometimes the controls on an app or Web page are not labeled appropriately. For example, a student may be using a math app where the developer of the app has not labeled the button used to check the answers correctly. In that case, the student would hear a generic label such as "button" rather than the appropriate "check answer" label. Working with a sighted person, it is possible for a student to rename an item so that it has a more descriptive label. To rename the label, the student will first select the button that has been incorrectly labeled (this may require some help from a sighted partner), and then double-tap and hold with two fingers. This will bring up a dialogue box where the student can enter the desired label for the button. When finished entering the name for the new label, the student will select Save and double-tap. VoiceOver will then read the custom label created by the student each time the button is selected in the app.

Entering and Editing Text

Entering and editing text can be somewhat difficult for people with visual disabilities on touch-screen devices because these devices rely on an onscreen keyboard for text entry rather than a tactile one. However, Apple has recognized that this can be a problem for people with visual disabilities and has created a special mode for typing called Touch Typing. With the standard typing mode on iOS, the user has to first select a character on the onscreen keyboard with one finger then tap on another area of the screen to input that character. This is known as split-tapping. With Touch Typing, the user selects a character on the onscreen keyboard and waits for VoiceOver to provide feedback by speaking the selected character aloud. When the user hears the character, he or she can just lift a finger and the character will be entered. This mode of entering text can be much faster and easier to learn for new VoiceOver users. To help with accuracy, VoiceOver can read the suggestions made by the auto-correct feature as you type if you enable Speak Auto-correct in your device's Settings.

Another major improvement in this area was the introduction of a new Dictation feature with the third-generation iPad. The dictation feature allows the user to enter text by speaking to the device, and it can save a lot of time and effort. Using this Dictation feature, a student can type a paper in a fraction of the time it would take to do so with either one of the two typing modes supported by VoiceOver.

To dictate text on your iPad, do the following:

1. Navigate to a text box where you would enter text. This should launch the onscreen keyboard.
2. Select the Dictate button (to the left of the Space Bar) on the onscreen keyboard and double-tap with one finger. A tone will indicate that the device is in listening mode.
3. Speak the desired text into the microphone at the top of your iPad.
4. When finished speaking the desired text, double-tap with two fingers to end the dictation.

To watch a brief tutorial showing you how to use the Dictation feature with VoiceOver, visit http://bit .ly/DictationVoiceOver or scan QR Code 5.5.

QR Code 5.5
Using
VoiceOver
With Dictation

Using a Wireless Keyboard With VoiceOver

You can also enter text on your iPad with a wireless keyboard while VoiceOver is running. To set up your keyboard to work with your iPad, you must enable Bluetooth:

1. Go into the Settings, choose General > Bluetooth and make sure Bluetooth is enabled.
2. Turn on the keyboard and wait for it to be recognized by your iPad. When the keyboard is recognized, it will appear under Devices.
3. Tap the keyboard's name to begin pairing it with your iPad. A prompt will provide you with directions.
4. Enter the numbers that appear on the prompt on your keyboard and press Return on the keyboard. Your keyboard will then be set up to work with your iPad.

For a complete list of keyboard shortcuts available for VoiceOver when a wireless keyboard is connected, please see Appendix B. Most of these keyboard shortcuts involve pressing the Control and Option keys on the keyboard. These two keys are known as the VoiceOver or VO keys. In addition to keyboard shortcuts that use the VO keys, the QuickNav feature available on the Mac is also supported. QuickNav is helpful if a student can only use VoiceOver with one hand. Instead of needing to press the VO keys before entering a keyboard shortcut, most of the actions for QuickNav only involve the arrow keys, which are arranged as an inverted T in the lower-right corner of an Apple keyboard. Appendix C also includes a list of the keyboard shortcuts that can be used when the keyboard is set to the QuickNav mode.

Starting with iOS 5, several single-key commands are also available when browsing a Web page in the Safari app with QuickNav turned on. These single-key commands can make it easier for students with visual disabilities to navigate Web content with VoiceOver. Pressing the single-key command will take the student to the next item of that type, and holding down the shift key while pressing the single-key command will take him to the previous item. For example, pressing "H" will move the student to the next heading, "L" to the next link, "T" to the next table, and so on. A complete list of these single-key commands is available in Appendix C.

QR Code 5.6 Using VoiceOver With a Wireless Keyboard

To learn how to set up and use a wireless keyboard with VoiceOver, watch a brief video tutorial by scanning QR Code 5.6 or by visiting http://bit.ly/VOKeyboard.

Using VoiceOver With Siri

Siri is the personal assistant available on the third-generation and later iPad. With iOS 6, you can use Siri to launch apps, schedule events in your calendar, set up reminders, and more. Siri combines speech recognition and artificial intelligence in a way that allows you to use natural speech to make your requests rather than a preset list of commands. There are two ways to activate Siri while VoiceOver is enabled on the iPad:

- Press and hold the Home button on your device until you hear the Siri tone, then ask a question or tell Siri what you want it to do.
- Press and hold the center button on your Apple headphones that have a microphone, then ask a question or tell Siri what you want it to do when you hear the tone.

VoiceOver Compatibility for Third-Party Apps

Not all apps are compatible with VoiceOver. While VoiceOver support is built into the Apple apps that ship with the iPad (Mail, Safari, etc.), third-party apps support will depend on how well the developer has followed Apple's suggested best practices for developing accessible apps. A great Web site to check the level of VoiceOver support for an app is AppleVis (www.applevis.com). Two of my favorite sections on this site are the App Directory and the list of most recommended apps. The list of most recommended apps shows the apps that have received the highest number of recommendations by AppleVis members, and the App Directory allows you to browse the app reviews submitted by AppleVis members by category (such as education, entertainment, social networking, etc.). I would also recommend the ViA app from the Braille Institute. This is an app designed to help blind and low-vision users sort through the many apps in the App Store to locate apps that have been specifically created for blind and low-vision users.

Apps for VoiceOver Users

The apps in this section have been designed for people who have little or no remaining functional vision. These apps can help VoiceOver users navigate their surroundings, perform a number of everyday tasks (counting money, identifying groceries, etc.), and access and manage information (reading e-books, listening to podcasts, and reading services, creating to do lists, etc.).

- LookTel Money Reader

  $9.99

  Money Reader quickly recognizes currency and speaks the denomination aloud. The app uses object recognition to allow people with visual disabilities to easily identify and count paper currency, including the U.S., Canadian, and Australian dollars, the British Pound and the Euro. There is no configuration necessary to use this app. All that is required to recognize a bill is to wave it in front of the iPad's camera and its denomination will be announced almost instantaneously. The app will recognize the bill even if it is folded, and it does not require Internet access to work.

- LookTel Recognizer

  $9.99

  Recognizer builds on the same pattern recognition technology used by Money Reader to allow people with visual disabilities to use their iOS devices to identify everyday objects. Recognizer requires the user to first take photos of objects in order to build a database of the items that can be identified later when scanned with the camera on an iOS device, and this step requires sighted assistance.

- Digit-Eyes

$19.99

Digit-Eyes is a barcode reader app. It enables people with visual disabilities to scan UPC and EAN barcodes and hear the names of more than 25 million products, including groceries, office supplies, and more. Digit-Eyes can also be used to scan quick response (QR) codes like the ones found throughout this book. On the Digit-Eyes Web site (www.digit-eyes. com), you can create custom labels with QR codes that can be printed on inexpensive address labels at home. These custom labels can contain text to be read aloud (up to 100 characters) or a recorded audio message that can be played back whenever the QR code is scanned. You can also buy preprinted washable labels that can be sewn into garments to make them easier to identify. A free lite version of the Digit-Eyes app is also available. It can read labels with Digit-Eyes QR codes, but not UPC barcodes.

- TapTapSee

Free

This app uses advanced pattern recognition to recognize objects when a photo is taken with the iPad's built-in camera. The app is designed for people with visual impairments, and VoiceOver needs to be turned on to hear the app announce when an object has been identified.

- VizWiz

Free

The idea behind the VizWiz app is to use the collective intelligence of the Web to provide people with visual disabilities with accurate information about their surroundings. The VizWiz app allows you to take a photo of any object and record a question that can be answered over the Internet by a volunteer known as a Web worker. You also can send out your request via email to people in your contacts list, or submit it through

Twitter or Facebook where it can be answered by any of your followers or friends. The app is fully compatible with the VoiceOver screen reader.

- oMoby

Free

The oMoby app was designed as a visual search app for shopping. The idea is that you can take a photo of any product to access shopping information for that product available on the Web. Since oMoby has support for VoiceOver, people with visual disabilities can use the app to identify products in their surroundings.

- Ariadne GPS

$5.99

Ariadne GPS provides talking maps that can be accessed with the VoiceOver screen reader. At any time, you can select "where am I?" and the app will announce your approximate location based on GPS coordinates. You can explore the area around you ("look around") or enter a different address to explore a remote location you plan to visit. When you touch a point on the map, after a short delay, the app will announce the street information. You can also save favorite locations, and the app will announce when you are close to them (with a sound, vibration, or vocal alert). One thing to note about Ariadne GPS is that the app relies on online mapping services that can become unresponsive at times. As the developer notes, the aim of the app is to give people with visual disabilities an idea of their position and what is around them, but the app should not be relied on completely for navigation.

- Sendero GPS LookAround

$4.99

With Sendero GPS, people with visual disabilities can use VoiceOver to announce the current street, the nearest current street, and nearby points of interest.

- Light Detector

$0.99

This is a simple app that emits a sound that will intensify as you approach a light source. It can be helpful for finding windows and exits quickly.

- Voice Brief

  $2.99

  I call this app my daily briefing. Every morning, I use this app to listen to my new email messages, the latest messages in my Twitter and Facebook feeds, and the weather. I find it a great way to start the day with the information I need. While this app was not designed for people with visual disabilities, its interface is accessible with the VoiceOver screen reader, and it includes its own high-quality voices to read information aloud.

- List Recorder

  $0.99

  List Recorder is a VoiceOver-compatible app for making lists that can include text, audio recordings, or both.

- Chime

  Free

  Chime is an app that provides an audible alert or chime on the hour, half hour, or quarter hour to help someone with a visual disability keep track of time. The alert can be one of three chirp sounds, or one of two simulated human voice (male or female).

- Vokul

  $2.99

  Using simple voice commands, Vokul allows a VoiceOver user who does not have the Siri personal assistant on his or her iPad to dictate emails and post to Twitter and Facebook. The app also can also be used to control playback in many of the media apps available for the iPad. Examples of Vokul commands include, "Hey Vokul update my Facebook status," or "Hey Vokul play sonata in F major."

- Read2Go

  $19.99

  Through a special grant from the U.S. Department of Education, any student who has a documented visual disability can qualify for Bookshare services. Bookshare members can use the Read2Go app to access e-books in the DAISY format. This is a format for talking books that also have flexible navigation options (such as by page, paragraph, sentence, or word). With Read2Go, students with visual disabilities can choose to hear a DAISY book read aloud by one of the two high-quality Acapela voices (male and female) included with the app. The app has support for the VoiceOver screen reader, and it can be used with a Bluetooth braille display.

- Learning Ally

  Free

  Formerly known as Recordings for the Blind and Dyslexic, Learning Ally is a membership service that provides access to a library of more than 70,000 audiobooks read by real people rather than a computer voice. Membership is $99 a year, and it requires proof of a print disability, such as a visual impairment. The Learning Ally Audio app has options for changing the speaking rate, bookmarking important passages, and navigating by chapter or page number. The app is also compatible with the VoiceOver screen reader.

- Podcasts

  Free

  Podcasts is an Apple app for subscribing and listening to podcasts. Like other Apple apps, Podcasts is compatible with VoiceOver.

- Downcast

  $1.99

  Downcast is a VoiceOver-compatible app for subscribing and listening to podcasts.

- iBlink Radio

  Free

  This app from Serotek Corporation can be used to access a number of reading services that provide narration of newspapers, magazines, and other print publications, including *USA Today*, the *New York Times*, and the *Wall Street Journal*. The app also has a community radio section that features stations owned or operated by people with limited or no eyesight, as well as a podcasts section with podcasts produced by individuals with visual disabilities.

- TweetList Pro

  $2.99

  AppleVis community members have rated TweetList Pro as the most accessible Twitter client for VoiceOver users. I have included this app on this list because I believe access to social media is important for allowing people with visual disabilities to reach out to not only other people with visual disabilities who are online, but nondisabled peers with similar interests as well.

To download the apps mentioned in this section, visit http://pinterest.com/mlearning4all/apps-for-voiceover-users/.

Practice Activities

1. Turn on VoiceOver in the Accessibility preferences for your device, and then use the VoiceOver practice area to practice some of the basic gestures. (Hint: Select VoiceOver Practice and double-tap.)
2. Using only VoiceOver gestures, exit the VoiceOver practice mode and return to the main VoiceOver settings screen.
3. Wait a few seconds to let the screen sleep, then practice unlocking the device. (Hint: Select Slide to Unlock and double-tap.)
4. With VoiceOver still turned on, turn on the screen curtain (three finger tap) and leave the screen turned off for the rest of this practice session.
5. Use one of the gestures you just learned (Hint: three fingers) to scroll down one page in the VoiceOver screen.
6. Practice changing some of the VoiceOver settings:

   - Select Speaking Rate and practice using a standard gesture (Hint: It involves a hold) to adjust the speaking rate to 35 percent.
   - Set the typing feedback for both keyboards (software and hardware) to words, and then turn on Use Phonetics and Use Pitch Change.
   - Open the Rotor screen and make sure headings, links, and forms are included in the Web Rotor.
   - Change the Language Rotor to include Spanish (Español) and Italian (Italiano).

7. Return to the Accessibility screen and set the Triple-Click Home button to Toggle VoiceOver.

8. Return to your Home screen and practice moving your finger across the top of the screen: What is your signal strength? What is the time? What is your battery status?

9. Move to the Spotlight screen (Hint: three fingers) and practice typing "Safari." (Hint: split tap) When the results are read back, select Safari and open the app.

10. When Safari opens, move the VoiceOver cursor to the Google Search field. This time use the rotor gesture to select Typing Mode and choose Touch Typing. (Hint: Tap a letter and release.) Enter "iPad" in the search field, and then select Search on the keyboard.

11. When the results page opens, use the rotor to select Links and practice navigating the page using just the links.

12. Follow one of the links, and then use the rotor to select Headings and navigate the page using only the headings.

13. Go back to the Spotlight screen (Hint: Click the Home button a few times) and type iBooks. Open the app and practice the reading gestures (read from top, read from current location, or stop reading). Practice using the rotor to change the language and speaking rate.

14. Exit the iBooks app and practice navigating the screens. (Hint: Three fingers)

15. If you have an Apple wireless keyboard, take some time to practice both modes of navigation: using the VO keys and with QuickNav. To help you learn the shortcuts as you practice, turn on the VoiceOver keyboard help with the keyboard (VO + K). When you are finished with your practice session, press the Escape key to exit the VoiceOver keyboard help.

16. Turn off the screen curtain.

17. Triple-click Home to turn off VoiceOver.

Supports for Students With Low Vision

Zoom

Checkpoint 1.1—Offer ways of customizing the display of information.

For those with low vision, Apple mobile devices support two ways of making the items on the screen easier to see:

- The pinch gesture can be used to zoom in and out on specific elements in apps that support this gesture, such as Mail or Safari. With this pinch gesture, you can enlarge an image or zoom in on the text. In the Safari app, you can also double-tap on some items to make them fit the screen.

- The Zoom feature makes it possible to magnify the entire screen. This feature works everywhere, including the Unlock and Spotlight screens and third-party apps purchased in the App Store.

Most of the gestures for using the Zoom feature use three fingers:

- Three-finger double-tap zooms in and out (the default setting is to zoom up to 200%).
- Three-finger double-tap and hold, and then drag up or down will change the magnification. You can zoom up to 500%.
- Three-finger drag while zoomed in to move around the screen.
- Touch one finger near the edge of the screen while zoomed in will pan (move) the display.

To use these gestures you will first have to activate the Zoom feature in the Settings app (under General > Accessibility > Zoom). If you plan to use Zoom a lot, you may want to set your Triple-Click Home shortcut to include it as one of the options.

Even though the Zoom feature is intended for people with low vision, this feature can be a useful teaching tool. For example, if you have a large class you can zoom in on the content so that students in the back of the classroom can see it better. You can also use this feature when you want students to focus on a specific part of the content. For example, while showing off a complex equation in a math class, you could use Zoom to have students focus on the first equation to be solved before moving to the next step of the problem. In this way, you can break down a complex problem into small steps that can appear less overwhelming to students. In a science class where you want to show a complex diagram, you can use Zoom to focus on specific parts of the diagram while you discuss them with the class, and then you could zoom out to help students see the relationship of the parts to the whole. In a social studies class, you could use Zoom to show a more detailed view on a map. When showing students how to use software in a technology class, you can use Zoom to more clearly point out where students should click. With Web sites, you could use Zoom to hide some of the advertisements that might distract students from the rest of the content.

QR Code 5.7
Zoom Feature
of iOS

To view a brief tutorial that shows how to use the Zoom feature, scan QR Code 5.7 or visit http://bit.ly/iOSZoom.

Large Text

Checkpoint 1.1—Offer ways of customizing the display of information.

This feature changes the size of the text in supported applications, such as Notes, Contacts, Mail, and Messages. The text size setting starts at 20 point and goes up to 56 point in increments of eight. This feature is found under General > Accessibility > Large Text in the Settings.

Invert Colors

Checkpoint 1.1—Offer ways of customizing the display of information.

This feature will invert the colors on the screen and provide higher contrast for people with low vision. The higher contrast can also benefit other students when they use their iPads in bright lighting. For example, if the students take their iPads on a field trip where they have to document what they see and experience during the trip, turning on Invert Colors may reduce the glare and make use of the device while outdoors less tiring for their eyes. To enable this feature choose General > Accessibility in the Settings and tap the On/Off switch for Invert Colors. You can also enable this feature by including as one of the options for Triple-Click Home. Invert Colors works throughout iOS, including the Unlock screen, the Spotlight search screen, and even while using Zoom and VoiceOver.

Speak Selection

Checkpoint 2.3—Support decoding text, mathematical notation, and symbols.

This feature introduced in iOS 5 will let you hear selected text using the same voice as VoiceOver. Speak Selection is for people with low vision who do not yet need fulltime use of a screen reader. To use this feature, you will first need to enable it in the Settings by going to General > Accessibility > Speak Selection and tapping the On/Off switch. Once the feature is enabled, select some text and tap Speak to hear it read aloud. In iOS 6, Speak Selection supports word highlighting as well as a number of dialects.

Speak Selection can be helpful not only for those with vision challenges, but for auditory learners, English language learners, and those learning how to read. For struggling readers, listening to text as it is read aloud can help these students with decoding by modeling pronunciation of letter and word sounds and by making a connection between oral language and written text. For English language learners, listening to the text to speech can help them learn the correct pronunciation of new words and build vocabulary. With both groups, iPads can be used to set up stations where students practice their language skills independently by first listening to the content read aloud by the text-to-speech voice and then recording themselves using the Voice Memos or another recording app. The teacher can then use these recordings to assess how well each student is progressing in their language acquisition. A similar activity could be used with foreign language students who need help with vocabulary.

QR Code 5.8
Speak
Selection
Feature of iOS

To watch a video tutorial showing the new features of Speak Selection in iOS 6, scan QR Code 5.8 or visit http://bit.ly/SpeakSelection.

Apps for Students With Low Vision

The apps in this section are for people who still have some functional vision and, thus, may not yet need to use the VoiceOver screen reader. One thing to consider when using some of these apps is the quality of the camera. You will generally get better results if you are using a third-generation iPad or later because of the better cameras in those devices.

- Over 40 Magnifier and Flashlight

  $1.99

  This app has support for magnification from 1X to 10X. While the free version of the app has ads, these can be removed with an in-app purchase. Note that the iPad does not have an LED Flash like the iPhone, thus, you cannot use the flashlight feature of this app on the iPad.

- Jumbo Calculator

  Free

  This is an alternative to the built-in calculator app that has large buttons for people with low vision.

- Talking Calculator

  $1.99

  Talking Calculator is a calculator app with speech support and a high-contrast view (bright-yellow background with black buttons and white text). The speech feature can also be helpful for people with dyscalculia.

- Alarm Clock HD

  $0.99

  My favorite alarm clock app has a high contrast display, and you can customize it by selecting your favorite bright color in the settings. Another feature is the ability to double-tap on the screen to turn the iPad screen white, effectively making it a flashlight. The entire interface has a dark background with high contrast text, making this app easy to use for people with low vision. In addition to using this app as a nightstand clock app, you can set alarms and timers with your own music.

- Glow Draw

  Free

  Glow Draw is a drawing app with bright neon colors that can be useful for presenting information to children who have low vision. The color and brush size can be changed by tapping a button at the bottom of the screen, and the app supports importing an image from the Camera Roll to trace over it.

- VisionSim

  Free

  VisionSim is an app from the Braille Institute that can make it easier for a person with low vision to explain their condition to others. The app uses the iPad's camera and an overlay to demonstrate what each visual disability is like. You can use a slider to adjust the level of vision loss shown, and tapping Learn More will open a page with additional information about the visual disability.

To download the apps mentioned in this section, visit http:// pinterest.com/mlearning4all/low-vision/.

Practice Activities

1. Open the Accessibility settings on your iPad and select Zoom.
2. Turn Zoom on and practice the various zoom gestures (quickly zoom in and out, move around the screen while zoomed in, and change the zoom level).

3. Set Large Text to 40 point. Open the Mail app and take a look at the text. Is it easier to read?

4. In Settings, turn Speak Selection on and make sure word highlighting is selected.

5. Open the Safari app and browse to a page with some text you can select. Double-tap the text to select, and choose Speak to hear it read aloud.

6. Go back into Settings and practice changing the dialect for the English voice. Go back to the Web page you opened in Safari and use Speak Selection to hear the text read aloud with a different dialect.

6

Auditory Supports

This chapter focuses on the accessibility features of the iPad for students with hearing difficulties. While the iPad does not include as many built-in accessibility features for hearing as the iPhone, it does support a number of apps that facilitate communication for students with hearing difficulties. Apple's FaceTime video chat technology, which is supported on the iPad, provides a convenient means of communication for students who rely on sign language to communicate. Similarly, the Messages app facilitates communication between students with hearing difficulties and their hearing peers using a medium (texting) that is familiar to both. Along with these communication apps, the iPad features support for closed-captioning. As the use of videos in the classroom continues to rise, this support for closed-captioning can help ensure students with hearing difficulties are not left out from being able to access the content in these videos.

Universal Design for Learning (UDL) Guidelines

- *Multiple and Flexible Means of Representation:* Closed-captions provide another representation for audio information that not only benefits people who are deaf but, as noted previously, also other groups (English language learners, struggling readers, etc.).

- *Multiple and Flexible Means of Expression:* The FaceTime app makes it possible for deaf students to collaborate with one another by using video chat to communicate with sign language. The Messages app makes it easier for those students to communicate with hearing peers using a popular technology (texting) embraced by many young people.
- *Multiple and Flexible Means of Engagement:* The availability of closed-captions makes it possible for students with hearing disabilities to have access to movies, video podcasts, and other content that can be used to provide alternative representations (a movie or videotaped reenactment instead of just the text). As the use of video content in the classroom continues to grow, it is important to ensure students with hearing disabilities are not left out from accessing this content due to a lack of captions.

Mono Audio

Checkpoint 1.2—Offer alternatives for auditory information.

The one built-in accessibility feature available on the iPad for people with hearing loss is Mono Audio. When Mono Audio is enabled, the left and right channels of stereo audio will be combined into a mono signal played on both earpieces of your headphones. This enables someone with a hearing loss in one ear to hear the audio content from both channels with the other ear. To enable this feature, choose General > Accessibility in the Settings and tap the On/Off switch for Mono Audio. You can use the slider to adjust the volume level for each earpiece. Moving the slider to the left will make the audio on the left earpiece louder, and moving it to the right will do the same for the right earpiece. This feature is helpful if you have a hearing loss that affects only one ear and you want to boost the volume for the audio in that ear while listening to a podcast or a movie for class.

FaceTime

Checkpoint 1.2—Offer alternatives for auditory information.
Checkpoint 5.2—Use multiple media for communication.
Checkpoint 8.3—Foster collaboration and communication.

FaceTime is the video chat app for iOS devices that have a forward-facing camera (which includes every iPad since the iPad 2). A version of FaceTime is also available for the Mac and can be used for video chat between an iPad and a computer. FaceTime is especially helpful for those who are deaf or who have a hearing loss because it allows them to use sign language to communicate over video chat. Students who are deaf can use FaceTime to collaborate on school projects, or a teacher who can sign can use it to communicate with students when they are home sick or with a parent who is deaf.

To use FaceTime on the iPad, you need to have an Apple ID. Originally, FaceTime calls could only be made over a Wi-Fi connection. Depending on your carrier and the data plan you have selected, with iOS 6, these calls can also be made over a cellular connection. To set up FaceTime on your iPad do the following:

1. Choose Settings > FaceTime.

Figure 6.1   FaceTime Option in the Settings

2. Enter your Apple ID information and tap Sign In. If you do not have an Apple ID, you can tap Create new Apple ID and follow the prompts to create one.

Figure 6.2   FaceTime Sign-In Screen in Settings

3. Once you are signed in with your Apple ID, select the email addresses other people should use to contact you with FaceTime, and then tap Next.

You can perform the same setup by launching the FaceTime app and following the prompts on the right side of the screen to enter your Apple ID and choose the email addresses other people will use to contact you with FaceTime.

To start a video call using the FaceTime app on your iPad, do the following:

1. Open the FaceTime app and sign in to FaceTime using your Apple ID.
2. Choose Contacts on the right side of the screen and tap the name of the contact you want to call. You will then see that contact's information. A camera icon next to a phone number or email address will indicate that the contact is available for a FaceTime call using that phone number or email address.

Figure 6.3   FaceTime Button for a Contact in the FaceTime App

3. Tap the desired phone number or email address to start the call.
4. When you're finished with the call, tap End at the bottom of the screen. To restart the call with the same contact, tap the Recents pane. This pane will show any calls you have recently made.
5. If you want to add a contact as a favorite, tap Favorites, then the plus (+), and select the contact from the list.

You can also start a FaceTime call from the Contacts app:

1. Open the Contacts app and tap the name of the person you want to call.
2. Choose FaceTime in the area below that person's contact information.

Figure 6.4   FaceTime Button for an Entry in the Contacts

3. Choose an email address the person you're calling uses to sign in to FaceTime (one with a camera icon next to it). FaceTime will then try to establish a connection.

Figure 6.5   Popover for Selecting a Number for the FaceTime Call

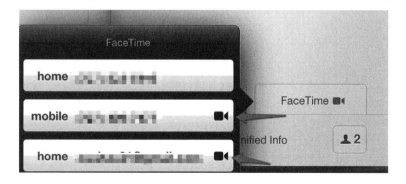

While you are on a FaceTime call, you will see yourself in a small window while the person you are speaking to will fill the rest of the screen. You can move the small window if it gets in the way. You can also switch between the forward facing camera and the one in the back of your iPad if you want to show the person on the call your surroundings. To do this, tap the Swap button at the bottom of the screen (to the right of the End button). You can also mute the microphone if you are only communicating with sign language by tapping the mute button to the left of End.

Figure 6.6   A Conversation in FaceTime

Messages and iMessages

Checkpoint 1.2—Offer alternatives for auditory information.
Checkpoint 5.2—Use multiple media for communication.
Checkpoint 8.3—Foster collaboration and communication.

The Messages app provides a convenient way for those with hearing disabilities to communicate with the rest of the world by sending and receiving text messages. Like FaceTime, you must first set up the Messages app with an Apple ID in Settings. Once you are signed in with your Apple ID, you can launch the Messages app, type your text message, and tap Send to start a conversation.

iMessages is not a separate app, but rather an add-on to the Messages app that only works for communication between Apple devices. When on a Wi-Fi connection, messages sent with iMessages will not count against your text messaging plan. This could be important if your text messaging plan does not offer unlimited data. With iMessages, you can send text messages that can also include photos, movies, and other information, such as a location in the Maps app or a contact from the Contacts app.

To send a message with iMessages, do the following:

1. Open the Messages app and tap the Write icon in the upper-right corner (a square with a pencil on it).

Figure 6.7   Button for Composing a New Message in the Messages App

2. Start typing the name of a contact and select from one of the suggestions, or tap the plus (+) to select one of your contacts in the Contacts app. You can confirm that your contact is using iMessages by the color of the Send button. If the button is blue, then the message will be sent using iMessages.

Figure 6.8   Send Button in Messages App

3. Enter the desired message text in the text field. The placeholder text in the text field should say, "iMessage," to let you know that you are sending a message using the iMessages service, and the keyboard should open automatically when you tap inside the text field.

4. If you want to send a photo or a movie, tap the camera icon to the left of the text field and select Take Photo or Video (to use the camera) or Choose Existing (to select a photo or movie from your Camera Roll).
5. Tap Send and your message will be sent to all recipients. The iMessages app supports group messages, so you can send a message to several contacts, and everyone will be able to participate in the conversation. You will see a visual indication when your recipients are typing a reply (a text bubble with dots inside).

Even if you close the Messages app, you can be alerted when a new message comes through in the Notifications Center. Simply swipe down with one finger from the top of the screen to see a list of incoming messages, and then tap any message to open it in the Messages app and write your reply.

To make communication even easier, the Messages app supports auto-correction to speed up text entry. This feature is enabled by default, but if you need to enable it after it has been turned off, choose Settings > General > Keyboard and tap the On/Off switch for auto-correction.

To use auto-correction, do the following:

1. Begin typing a word and continue until you see a suggestion.
2. To accept the suggestion, press the space bar and continue on to the next word.
3. To reject the suggestion, finish typing the word as you want it to appear in your message, and then tap the "X" to dismiss the suggestion before you start the next word.

Figure 6.9   Example of an Auto-Correct Suggestion in the Messages App

Support for Closed-Captions

Checkpoint 1.2—Offer alternatives for auditory information.
Checkpoint 2.2—Clarify syntax and structure.
Checkpoint 2.4—Promote understanding across languages.
Checkpoint 2.5—Illustrate through multiple media.

Closed-captions allow someone who has a hearing impairment to follow the action onscreen by reading text of the dialogue and any sounds that are essential for understanding. To enable closed-captions on your iPad, choose Video in the Settings and set the switch for Closed-Captioning to On. This will enable the captions for all videos that include them. You are not able to control the display of captions on individual videos.

To create your own closed-captioned content, you can use programs such as MovieCaptioner (Synchrimedia), World Caption (University of Wisconsin-Madison), or MacCaption (Computer Prompting and Captioning Company). Of these three products, I have found MovieCaptioner to provide the combination of low cost and ease of use that should meet the needs of most educators. MovieCaptioner will open a QuickTime movie and let you loop through a few seconds of video while you type the captions. To create a file that is compatible with mobile devices, your video file should be in the .m4v file type before you open it for captioning with MovieCaptioner. This file type can be selected as an export option in iMovie, Final Cut, or QuickTime. When you're finished entering all of the captions, choose Export > Sonic Scenarist (SCC Embed in QT) in MovieCaptioner to create a file that includes closed-captions.

Adding Closed-Captions to Videos for iBooks

Checkpoint 1.2—Offer alternatives for auditory information.

The videos in iBooks textbooks can include closed-captions. To view these captions when you open the book on the iPad, you need to make sure "Show closed-captions" is selected in the Settings. However, not all captioned videos are supported in iBooks textbooks. To create a captioned video that is compatible with iBooks, I have found that a workflow combining MovieCaptioner (available from www.synchrimedia.com for $99) and Compressor (available

QR Code 6.1
Closed-
Captioning
a Video for
iBooks Author
With Movie-
Captioner

on the Mac App Store for $50) works well. With MovieCaptioner, I create an SCC file that has the caption text and time codes. I then use Compressor to combine this SCC file with the original video file, resulting in a captioned version of the video. Compressor also helps me make sure the captioned video file is in the correct format for the iPad. I found that when I exported the captioned video directly from MovieCaptioner, I would get an error message in iBooks Author, and the software would refuse to import the video. To learn more about how to create captions for iBooks textbooks with MovieCaptioner, you can scan QR Code 6.1 to view a video tutorial, or visit http://bit.ly/ClosedCaptions.

Apps for Students With Hearing Loss

- SoundAMP R

$4.99

While I mentioned this app in the learning and literacy chapter for its recording capabilities that can be used for note taking, SoundAMP R is really a sound amplification app that can be used to amplify classroom sounds for a student who has a difficult time hearing the teacher or other students. While wearing headphones, the student can use sliders to tune the sound for different frequencies in either the center, left, or right sides of the sound field. A Zoom slider filters out background sounds to allow the student to hear the teacher or another speaker more clearly or to focus on background sounds when it can be helpful for safety. SoundAMP R supports multitasking, making it possible to continue using the app even after switching to another task on the device (surfing the Web, answering emails, etc.). The app can record the last 30 seconds of audio in the background. This is helpful for a student who has missed something important the teacher has said in class. A quick tap of the Replay button and the student can listen to what was said again.

- Awareness

$6.99

Awareness is another sound amplification app that works with the inline microphone on the iPhone headphones. Awareness feeds the ambient sound into your headphones and amplifies it so it is easier to hear. VoiceOver support for students with both hearing and visual disabilities can be added to the app with an in-app purchase of $0.99.

- Dragon Dictation

Free

A hearing person can use Dragon dictation to communicate with someone who has a hearing loss by converting his or her speech to text with this app. The person with the hearing loss can type answers using the onscreen keyboard. While not perfect, this method of communication can be helpful in a pinch when no other options are available.

- IP-Relay

Free

IP-Relay, from Purple, enables people who are deaf or who have hearing loss to use an iPad to call people who are hearing. Like an instant messaging chat, you type your side of the conversation and a certified IP-Relay operator receives it and voices everything you type to the hearing person. When the hearing person responds, the operator types her or his words back to you. The IP-Relay service is a federally funded resource for all qualified people who are deaf or who have a hearing loss, so there is no charge for calls and they do not count against your minutes.

- Purple VRS

Free

Similar to IP-Relay, Purple VRS is a video-based telephone relay system for people who are deaf or who have a hearing loss. VRS calls can be made over a Wi-Fi or 3G connection.

- Skype

  Free

  Skype allows students with hearing disabilities to make video calls to other students or their teacher to communicate with sign language. Calls to any Skype user are free over a Wi-Fi or 3G connection. An advantage of using Skype is that it is a cross-platform service (Windows, Mac, Android, and iOS), whereas FaceTime only works on Apple devices (Macs and iOS devices).

- Fring

  Free

  Fring is a video chat app that allows up to four people to participate in a group video call, which is great for collaboration on school projects for all students, but even more so for students with hearing disabilities who must use sign language to communicate. The app, which supports free text messaging and phone calls to other Fring users over Wi-Fi, 3G, and 4G connections, is available for both iOS and Android devices.

To download the apps mentioned in this chapter, please visit http://pinterest.com/mlearning4all/hearing/.

Practice Activities

1. Find one of your favorite audio programs (podcast, audio book, etc.) and take a few turns listening to the content with only one earpiece while you turn Mono Audio on and off. What would you miss if you did not have this option?
2. While you have Mono Audio turned on, play that same audio program with both earpieces and use the slider to adjust the volume on each side.
3. Start a new FaceTime call and practice communicating with a friend without using any sounds. Ask your friend to mute the microphone (and you do the same). Practice switching to the back camera on your device and showing your friend your current location.
4. Open the Messages app and send a message to one of your contacts (Note: data charges may apply). Wait for the other person to reply, and then send back a message with a photo or

a short video showing the other person your location. Was your message an iMessage or a traditional text message? How do you know?

5. Search for a closed-captioned podcast on iTunes U on your Mac. Download an episode of the podcast on iTunes and sync your device.

6. Turn on the support for captions on your device and spend a few minutes watching the new episode you just downloaded with the volume turned down.

7

Motor Supports

Some disabilities make it difficult for people to operate the physical buttons on a mobile device. The touch screen interface on the iPad can make this device easier to use for people with such motor difficulties. To take advantage of that interface, Apple introduced a feature called AssistiveTouch that allows people with motor difficulties to access many of the device functions controlled by physical buttons by tapping on icons that appear on the screen instead. AssistiveTouch is also helpful to someone using the device in a wheelchair, where the device may be on a mount and the person may not be able to easily access the buttons. Furthermore, new technologies such as Siri, which is intended to make hands-free operation easier for everyone, can also benefit people with motor disabilities.

Universal Design for Learning (UDL) Guidelines

- *Multiple and Flexible Means of Action and Expression:* The accessibility features in this section provide options for expression by allowing children who struggle with typing to show what they know by other means (such as by using their voice to dictate the information). Other features such as AssistiveTouch make it easier for children with motor difficulties to operate and navigate their mobile devices.

Siri

Checkpoint 4.1—Vary the methods for response and navigation.

Siri is the personal assistant available on the third-generation or later iPad (with iOS 6). With Siri, you can use your voice to send messages, schedule appointments and reminders, and more. Siri combines speech recognition and artificial intelligence in a way that allows you to use natural speech rather than a preset list of commands. For example, you can say, "Tell my mom I will be home in ten minutes," and Siri will start a new text message with the text you just spoke. Siri is enabled by default on the devices that support it (any third-generation or later iPad), and it works with many of the built-in apps, such as Messages, Calendar, Reminders, and more. If Siri is disabled on your iPad, you can enable it by going to Settings > General > Siri and tapping the On/Off switch at the top of the screen.

There are two ways to activate Siri on the iPad once it is enabled in the Settings:

- Press and hold the Home button on your device until you hear the Siri tone, and then ask a question or tell Siri what you want it to do.
- Press and hold the center button on your Apple headphones that have a microphone, and then ask a question or tell Siri what you want it to do when you hear the tone.

These techniques for activating Siri may present a challenge depending on the kind of motor challenge a person has. For example, someone may not have the ability to press the Home button with enough strength or long enough to activate Siri as described previously. Fortunately, Siri can also be activated with the AssistiveTouch feature discussed later in this chapter.

If you ask Siri, "What can you do?" it will present a list of common things you can do with it. For example, students can use Siri to take notes ("Note that I have to include the following three things in my essay for English class"), search the Web ("Google War of 1812"), or perform simple calculations ("What is the square root of 128?"). Starting with iOS 6, Siri can launch apps (say, "Launch Mail" to open your email, or "Launch Camera" to open the Camera app).

Siri is currently available in only a few languages. To change to a different language, such as Australian or UK English, go to Settings > General > Siri > Language. Siri requires an active Internet connection to work.

Dictation

Checkpoint 4.1—Vary the methods for response and navigation.
Checkpoint 4.2—Optimize access to tools and assistive technologies.
Checkpoint 5.2—Use multiple tools for construction and composition.

On the third-generation or later iPad, the dictation feature can make it easier for people with typing difficulties to enter text. This feature is available anytime the onscreen keyboard is visible. To start dictating, tap the Dictate icon (a microphone) to the left of the space bar on the onscreen keyboard.

Figure 7.1   Dictation Button on the Onscreen Keyboard

No training to a specific user's voice is necessary for the dictation to work. You can use this feature to compose emails, text messages, short notes, and more. Tap Done when you're done with your dictation, and your text should appear in the appropriate text field or document. You can then use the onscreen keyboard to correct any mistakes. You should note that dictation will only work when Internet access is available.

AutoFill and Auto-Correction

Checkpoint 4.1—Vary the methods for response and navigation.

The AutoFill feature can save some time for students who have motor impairments by automatically filling out Web forms with their contact information. To enable this feature, choose Safari > AutoFill in the Settings, then set the switch for Use Contact Info to On. By tapping My Info, you can select the entry in your Contacts that will be used to fill out Web forms when you use Safari.

The Auto-Correction feature provides predictive text entry in apps such as Messages, Mail, and more. To enable Auto-Correction, do the following:

1. Go to Settings > General > Keyboard.
2. Set the switch for Auto-Correction to On.
3. Open your favorite editing app and start typing until you see a suggestion. To accept the suggestion, press the space bar on the onscreen keyboard. To reject the suggestion, tap the "X."

Custom Shortcuts

Checkpoint 4.1—Vary the methods for response and navigation.

The custom shortcuts feature can be used as an alternative to typing longer blocks of text. For example, you can create a "sig" shortcut that when entered will expand to your full email signature. Custom shortcuts can make it easier to enter text if you have motor difficulties. To create a custom shortcut, do the following:

1. Go to Settings > General > Keyboard.
2. Choose Add New Shortcut.
3. Enter the text to be inserted in the Phrase text field, and then enter an optional shortcut. If you do not enter a shortcut, the text will expand after you type the first few characters, in much the same way the auto-correction feature works.

QR Code 7.1
Custom
Shortcuts

To learn more about custom shortcuts, you can watch a brief video tutorial at http://bit.ly/CustomShortcuts, or you can scan QR Code 7.1.

AssistiveTouch and Custom Gestures

Checkpoint 4.1—Vary the methods for response and navigation.
Checkpoint 4.2—Optimize access to tools and assistive technologies.

AssistiveTouch was designed to make the iPad and other iOS devices easier to use for people with motor difficulties. For example, someone who is not able to press the Home button to exit an app can now open an overlay menu with icons for many of the hardware functions of the device, including the Home button. AssistiveTouch is also helpful if you have the device mounted on a stand or a wheelchair mount and cannot easily access the physical buttons on the device to perform actions such as raising and lowering the volume.

To use AssistiveTouch, do the following:

1. Choose Settings > General > Accessibility and turn on Assistive Touch. You will know assistive touch is enabled when you see a floating circular icon on the screen.

Figure 7.2   Floating Icon for AssistiveTouch

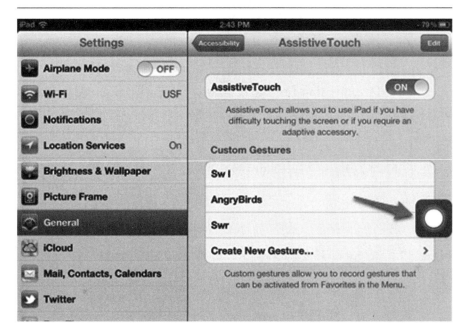

2. Tap the icon to open the overlay menu with the AssistiveTouch options. Note that you can move the AssistiveTouch icon to another area of the screen if it gets in the way.
3. Select an option from the overlay menu. If you're working with a gesture and want to select a different one, tap the floating AssistiveTouch icon again to return to the AssistiveTouch menu and select a different option.

The overlay menu for AssistiveTouch is organized into the following groups:

- Home: Tapping this icon is the equivalent of pressing the physical Home button on the device, which is the way you exit apps in iOS.

Figure 7.3   Home Option in Main Menu for AssistiveTouch

- Siri: Tapping this button activates the Siri personal assistant. On the iPad 2 (or the third-generation or later iPad if Siri is disabled), the Siri button is replaced by Gestures (discussed later).
- Device: This group includes options for raising and lowering the volume, locking the screen, rotating the screen, and muting the volume.

Figure 7.4   Options in the Device Menu for AssistiveTouch

Tapping the icon with the three dots will open another menu with options for taking a screenshot, opening the task switcher (to view a list of recently opened apps and switch apps), simulating a shake of the device (which can undo the last action), and performing multi-touch gestures.

Figure 7.5   Second-Level Menu for Device in AssistiveTouch

Tapping Gestures will open a third menu with options that allow someone who can only use one finger to perform multi-touch gestures that require from two to five fingers. For example, swiping from left to right with four fingers on the iPad will allow you to quickly switch apps. To perform this gesture with just one finger (instead of four), open the AssistiveTouch menu, tap Device > More (three dots) > Gestures, and select the icon with the four fingers on it. On the iPad 2 (or the third-generation or later iPad with Siri disabled), the Gestures option appears on the first level of the AssistiveTouch menu, above the option for Home.

Figure 7.6   Gestures Options in AssistiveTouch

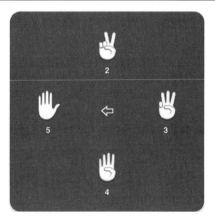

When you see the four blue dots on the screen, perform a swipe from one side of the screen with one finger and it will be the same as swiping with four fingers.

- Favorites: This group includes the pinch gesture used for zooming in or out on individual objects (not to be confused with the Zoom feature available in the accessibility settings that zooms the entire screen) as well any custom gestures you create.

Figure 7.7   Option for Pinch Gesture in Favorites Menu of
AssistiveTouch

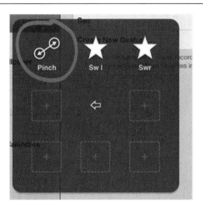

To use the zoom gesture, tap and drag on one of the handles with the arrow on it. When you're done, tap the AssistiveTouch icon a second time.

Figure 7.8   Using the Pinch Gesture With AssistiveTouch to Zoom in on a
Page of Text

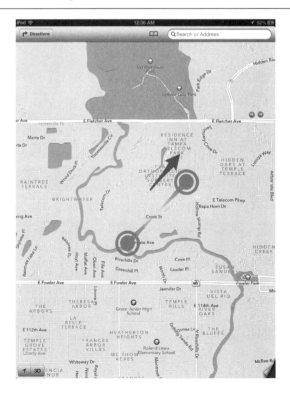

AssistiveTouch also supports custom gestures. To create a custom gesture, do the following:

1. Go to Settings > General > Accessibility > AssistiveTouch.
2. Choose Create New Gesture.

Figure 7.9   Creating a New Gesture in the AssistiveTouch Pane of the Settings

3. Perform the gesture by drawing with your finger on the screen, and then tap Stop.

Figure 7.10   Create a New Gesture by Drawing It on the Screen

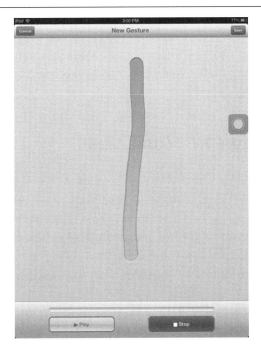

1. Tap Play to preview the custom gesture, and then Save if you're happy with the result.
2. Enter a name for the custom gesture and choose Save.

QR Code 7.2 Assistive-Touch Feature of iOS

The custom gesture will appear in the Favorites group of the AssistiveTouch menu. To perform the custom gesture, move the blue circle to the area of the screen where you want to perform the gesture and let go.

Scan QR Code 7.2 to watch a video that explains how to use AssistiveTouch, including how to create your own custom gestures. You can also access the video by visiting http://bit.ly/ATouch.

Switch Access

Checkpoint 4.2—Optimize access to tools and assistive technologies.

A switch device is an assistive technology device that can be used in place of a keyboard or mouse. A more detailed discussion of the switch access options available for iOS devices is available in Chapter 2. To use a switch with an iPad, it must first be connected to a Bluetooth interface that will communicate with the iPad wirelessly. This switch interface has to be paired with the iPad as follows:

1. Make sure the switch interface is turned on.
2. Go to Settings > General > Bluetooth.
3. Select the switch interface from the list shown on the iPad (you may be required to enter a pairing code with some interfaces).

With some switch interfaces that use the VoiceOver cursor to scan through the options on the screen (such as the Tecla Shield), you may have to enable VoiceOver as well.

Apps for Developing Fine Motor Skills

The apps in this section range from simple cause and effect apps to apps that focus on handwriting readiness. Many of the cause and effect apps listed here serve a dual purpose. First, they help children develop their understanding of cause and effect relationships, and second, they help children learn basic skills needed to interact with a touch screen device, such as tapping, flicking, and swiping gestures.

- iLoveFireworks

  $0.99

  When this app is open, touching the screen will display fireworks that vary in appearance and sound with each touch.

- Heat Pad

  $0.99

  Heat Pad is a free app that shows a heat print and plays a sound when you touch the screen. The bright colors should get the attention of children with autism.

- Fluidity

  Free

  Fluidity is a flow dynamics simulation that shows a swirling fluid pattern on the screen. Touching and dragging on the screen causes the colors to change. The bright colors in this app should make it attractive to children with autism.

- Fun Bubbles

  $0.99

  While there are many bubble apps on the App Store, what distinguishes Fun Bubbles is the variety of ways to make and pop the bubbles. Children not only learn how to perform a tapping motion on the touch screen but also how to tap and hold and how to hold and drag. Tapping the screen once creates a bubble, and tapping the bubble pops it. A tap and hold makes the bubble grow larger, but if the child holds too long, it pops. By holding and dragging, the child can also make a line of bubbles. A free lite version of the app is also available. The only difference between the lite and premium versions is that the premium version has options for changing the bubble color, speed controls, and changing the background with photos from the Camera Roll.

- Touch Trainer

  $4.99

  Touch Trainer provides practice with the touch response needed to use an iPad. The app plays music in the background, and it shows a simple animation whenever a button is touched for reinforcement. The button gets progressively smaller as the child moves through the levels. In the settings, the parent or caregiver can decide if the app should react to any touch or only to distinct taps.

- Toddler Sandbox

  $0.99

  Toddler Sandbox is a simple app that provides a picture the child has to erase by performing a swiping motion to reveal flashcards of common objects. In addition to developing motor skills, the app allows children to work on attention to the screen and basic vocabulary.

- Dexteria

  $4.99

  Dexteria is a set of therapeutic hand exercises that improves fine motor skills and handwriting readiness. Three types of exercises are included: Tap it provides practice with finger sequencing and isolation (the child must keep his or her thumb on one spot while tapping colored icons at varying distances from the other fingers), Pinch it provides practice with motor manipulation and control (the child must pinch to get rid of crabs that appear on the screen), and Write it improves finger control and stroke sequencing as the child traces letters on the screen. The app keeps track of the time spent on each section and the reports can be shared via email.

- iWriteWords

  $2.99

  The object of iWriteWords is to help Mr. Crab collect the numbered balls by dragging him with a finger to draw each letter. Children can practice drawing upper and lowercase letters as well as numbers. When they get all the letters, a drawing appears on the screen.

To download the apps mentioned in this section, visit http://pinterest.com/mlearning4all/fine-motor/.

Practice Activities

1. Launch Siri (on your third-generation or later iPad) and say, "What can you do?" to see a list of Siri commands. Practice using some of the commands shown: start a FaceTime call, send a text message, set an alarm, and so on.

2. Practice launching a few of the built-in apps with Siri if you have updated your iPad to iOS 6.

3. Practice using Siri to request information. For example, say, "What's the weather like?" to hear the weather for your location, or say, "Search the Web," followed by something you want to look up on the Web.

4. Send yourself an email message where you use the Dictation feature to enter text.

5. Create a custom shortcut for a favorite quote. Assign "quote" as the shortcut, and then open the Mail app and send yourself an email. In the body of the message, enter "quote" and press the space bar on the onscreen keyboard. What happened?

6. Turn on AssistiveTouch and open an app, and then practice exiting the app with AssistiveTouch. (Hint: Tap the Home icon)

7. Practice using the Device group in AssistiveTouch to raise and lower the volume, to rotate the screen, and finally, to lock the screen.

8. Practice using the options in the Gestures group in Assistive Touch to perform multi-finger gestures on your iPad: Open several apps, practice switching apps, and close an app using only AssistiveTouch multi-touch gestures.

9. Create a custom gesture that will let you swipe to change screens by performing a single tap and release on the screen.

8

Executive Functioning Supports

There are built-in apps in iOS, such as Reminders and Calendar that can help many effectively manage their life by making it easier to keep track of to-do lists, appointments, and other important information needed for day-to-day living. For all students with disabilities, the ability to act in a self-determined way (where they make their own decisions and manage their own lives) becomes an even more important goal as they approach adulthood. Children and adolescents who develop strong self-determination skills are more likely to be successful as adults who gain employment and enjoy greater social rewards (Wehmeyer, 2002). The apps in this chapter focus on planning and time management, two essential skills for living an independent, self-determined life. These apps can be especially helpful for students with disabilities, such as attention deficit hyperactivity disorder (ADHD), that affect executive function or their ability to perform activities such as planning, organizing, and managing time. I have also included in this chapter a number of other apps for independent living, including apps for learning about financial management for students who are employed.

Reminders

Checkpoint 6.1—Guide appropriate goal setting.
Checkpoint 6.2—Support planning and strategy development.
Checkpoint 6.3—Facilitate managing information and resources.

The Reminders app allows students to keep track of the various tasks they need to perform to successfully complete school assignments and achieve the personal goals they have set for themselves. The Reminders app has a simple design that makes it easy to learn and use, and it supports access with the VoiceOver screen reader. To create a new reminder, do the following:

1. Open the Reminders app and tap the Add (+) button.
2. Enter the desired description text for the reminder and tap Return on the onscreen keyboard. This will move you down to the next line so you can enter the next reminder. If you do not want to create additional reminders, dismiss the onscreen keyboard by tapping the key in the lower-right corner that looks like a keyboard.

Figure 8.1   Button for Hiding the Onscreen Keyboard on the iPad

3. Tap the reminder to edit its details.
4. For a reminder that will be triggered on a specific date, tap the On/Off switch for On a Day. Next, tap the date shown and use the spinners to select the exact date and time when you want the reminder to be triggered.

Figure 8.2   Creating a Reminder That Will Be Triggered at a Specific Date and Time

Tap Done when you're done selecting the date to return to the Details pane.

5. Tap Repeat to choose how often the reminder will repeat: every day, every week, every two weeks, every month, or every year. Tap Done when you have set the repeat interval to return to the Details pane.
6. Tap Priority to indicate the importance of the reminder (from low priority to high priority). Tap Done when you're done setting the priority to return to the Details pane.
7. Tap Show More to view additional details about the reminder.
8. If you have created lists to organize your reminders, tap List and choose the desired list for the reminder.
9. Tap Notes and enter any additional information about the reminder.
10. Tap Done to exit the Details pane and finish editing the reminder.
11. To mark the reminder as completed, tap the box next to its name.

Figure 8.3 Box for Indicating a Reminder Has Been Completed

12. To delete a reminder, tap its name and choose Delete at the bottom of the Details pane.

Students can use lists in the Reminders app to organize their reminders into useful categories (subjects, extracurricular activities, etc.). A completed list is available by default to help you keep track of those tasks you have already done. You switch lists by tapping on the name of a different list in the pane that appears on the left side of the screen. To create a new list, tap the Edit button in the upper-left corner of the screen, and then choose Create New List.

With iCloud, reminders can be updated between devices. To enable iCloud syncing for Reminders, go to Settings and choose iCloud, and then tap the On/Off switch for Reminders.

Calendar

Checkpoint 6.1—Guide appropriate goal-setting.
Checkpoint 6.2—Support planning and strategy development.
Checkpoint 6.3—Facilitate managing information and resources.

For students who find it difficult to keep track of due dates and other important deadlines, iOS has a built-in Calendar app that can help. The Calendar app has an intuitive interface that is also fully accessible with VoiceOver. To create a new event (such as an appointment or deadline) in the Calendar app, do the following:

1. Open the Calendar app and tap the Add (+) icon.
2. In the Title text field, enter a descriptive label for the event, and then indicate where it will take place in the location text field.
3. Tap Starts/Ends to enter a start and end time for the event. On the Start & End screen, use the date and time picker to choose the correct date and time, or tap the Off/On switch next to All-day to indicate the event will last an entire day.

Figure 8.4   Date and Time Picker for Selecting Start and End Times for an Event

4. Tap Done when you've entered the start and end information to return to the Add Event pane.
5. Tap each option under the date and time to enter additional details about the event (how often it will repeat, the people who are invited, when an alert will occur, which calendar it should be assigned to, and so on).

6. Use the Notes area at the bottom of pane to enter additional information about the event.
7. Tap Done in the Add pane to finish creating the event.

The Calendar app has a choice of views: day, week, month, and list. All of these views are accessible with VoiceOver.

With iCloud, you can keep your calendars up to date on all your devices. To enable iCloud syncing for your calendars, go to Settings > iCloud, and tap the On/Off switch for Calendars.

Clock

Checkpoint 6.1—Guide appropriate goal-setting.
Checkpoint 6.2—Support planning and strategy development.
Checkpoint 7.3—Minimize threats and distractions.

The Clock app, which was introduced on the iPad with iOS 6, provides another way to keep track of important events and deadlines by using alarms. To set up an alarm, do the following:

1. Open the Clock app, choose Alarm at the bottom of the screen, and tap the Add (+) button in the upper-right corner.
2. Choose Repeat and select how often the alarm will repeat, and then tap Back.
3. Choose Sound and select one of the sounds from the list. As you select each sound, you will be able to hear what it will sound like when the alarm comes on. Tap "Pick a song" if you would rather use a song from your music collection than a ringtone for the alarm. Tap Back when you're done making your selection.

Figure 8.5 Button to Pick a Song as Alarm Sound

4. Tap the On/Off switch for Snooze if you want to enable this option.
5. Tap Label and enter a descriptive label for the alarm (time to take medicine, etc.), then tap Back to return to the Add Alarm screen.
6. Use the time picker to choose the correct hours, minutes, and time of day (AM or PM) for the alarm, and then tap Save when you've entered all the information for the new alarm.

Figure 8.6   Time Selection for an Alarm

The Clock app's timer feature can be helpful for students who have a difficult time staying on task by letting them set goals to increase the amount of time they can maintain focus. To set a timer, do the following:

1. Open the Clock app and choose Timer.
2. Use the time picker to choose the number of hours and minutes for the timer.

Figure 8.7   Choosing the Duration for the Timer

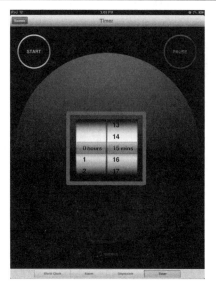

3. Tap Sounds in the upper-left corner, choose a ringtone that will play when the timer ends, and then tap Set.
4. Tap the Start button to start the timer.

Weather

Checkpoint 1.3—Offer alternatives for visual information.

The built-in Weather app is a quick way to find out what the weather outside is going to be like so you can dress appropriately. The app is especially helpful for people with visual disabilities because it is compatible with VoiceOver. It also has a simple layout and good contrast for people with low vision.

The information provided by the Weather app is also accessible with Siri on the third-generation or later iPad. To hear the weather, ask Siri, "What's the weather going to be like today?" or a similar question. Siri will then present a visual that shows the temperature and weather conditions (this visual is accessible with the VoiceOver screen reader).

In addition to the built-in weather app, another great option for weather information is iDress for Weather ($1.99, www.pebropro-ductions.com/idress-for-weather/). This app was specifically designed to support individuals whose cognitive processing or memory is affected by a disability (such as autism or other developmental disabilities) or has changed due to an injury or illness (such as a traumatic brain injury, stroke, Alzheimer's Disease, or dementia). The app has a clean, uncluttered interface and presents the weather information visually as a scene that represents the current weather conditions, with the temperature displayed at the top of the screen as a large, easy-to-see number. A unique feature of this app is that it will display the clothing that would be appropriate for the current weather conditions, and this clothing can be customized with images that represent students' personal clothing. They can also define personal interpretations of temperatures by customizing the parameters for hot, warm, cool, cold, and very cold in the settings.

Time Management Apps

Checkpoint 6.2—Support planning and strategy development.
Checkpoint 6.3—Facilitate managing information and resources.

In addition to the built-in Reminders, Calendar, and Clock apps, a number of third-party apps are available for helping students organize their daily lives through effective planning and time management.

- Wunderlist

  Free

  Wunderlist is a simple to-do list manager with cloud syncing capabilities. The advantage of using Wunderlist over the built-in Reminders app is that you will be able to sync your tasks across platforms. Wunderlist software is available for many platforms, including Windows computers and phones and Android tablets, or you can just use a Web browser to access your Wunderlist account on any device that has an Internet connection. To take advantage of some features built into Wunderlist, such as the reminders, you have to register for a free account. These reminders can be set up to be either a notification on your device or an email that gets sent to your Inbox.

- Agenda

  $0.99

  Agenda is a streamlined calendar app with gesture support. You can access each of the four views (day, week, month, and year) by swiping left or right with one finger. The week, month, and year views also scroll up and down to reveal more information (additional weeks, months, or years). Because Agenda simply provides a different view for the calendars set up in your iOS settings, you will not have to reenter the events you have set up in the built-in Calendar app if you decide to switch to Agenda. You can even simultaneously add events in both calendars if you prefer. The app also includes several themes, including a Blackout theme with higher contrast (dark background with light text).

- iStudiez Pro

  $2.99

  The app iStudiez Pro can help high school and college-age students manage and organize their academic schedules. The app can work with different types of schedules, including alternating (A and B weeks), rotating, and block schedules. For each course, the student can enter key information, including the instructor's name, contact information, and office hours. The app also has a special section for homework and assignments, with support for notifications to inform the student of due dates. One of their newest features allows the app to Cloud Sync, enabling it to synchronize data between iOS devices through the developer's servers. You can also back up your data by sending it out as an email attachment (clicking the attachment in your email will open iStudiez Pro and restore the data).

- Alarm Clock HD

  Free

  Alarm Clock HD is an alarm clock app with a high contrast display and alarms and timers that can be set up to use your own music.

- Time Timer

  $2.99

  Time Timer is a visual timer with a disappearing red disk to show the remaining time for a task. I will often use Time Timer when doing presentations to help me quickly see at a glance how much time I have left.

To download the time management apps mentioned in this section, visit http://pinterest.com/mlearning4all/time-management/.

Apps for Learning About Money Management

Checkpoint 6.1—Guide appropriate goal setting.

The following apps help students not only learn important money management skills but also work on their ability to set and manage personal goals. Financial literacy is especially important for older students who are either preparing for employment or who are already employed.

- Kids Money

  Free

  Kids Money teaches young children about saving and planning for long-term purchases. When the child wants to purchase an item, she or he enters the price along with expected weekly pocket money (from allowances, etc.) and any expected gift money. The app then helps the child figure out how long it will take to save enough money to purchase the item.

- P2K Money

  Free

  P2K Money teaches children to keep track of income like an allowance or payments for doing chores. Children can also create a wish list with photos of the items they would like to purchase.

- Bankaroo

  Free

  Bankaroo is a free Web-based service where parents can set up a virtual bank account to teach their children how to manage their allowance and other money.

You can download the financial literacy apps mentioned in this section by visiting http://pinterest.com/mlearning4all/financial-literacy/.

Practice Activities

1. Identify one important goal you want to accomplish in the following month, and then set a reminder for each task you need to complete to see that goal through.
2. Open the Calendar app and Identify three different points during the month when you will review your progress toward the goal you set in Step 1, and then create an alarm for each event to remind you of it the day before.
3. Think of one deadline you have over the next week. Set up an alarm to remind you of it.
4. Practice using the timer to engage in an activity (reading a book, meditating, etc.) for a set amount of time.
5. Think of your favorite city in the world you would like to visit. Now use the Weather app to look up the weather in that city. Practice finding the same information with Siri (on a third-generation or later iPad).

9

Managing iOS Devices in the Classroom

The first part of this chapter focuses on two features of iOS, Restrictions and Guided Access, that can help educators create a more focused learning environment for students by minimizing distractions while they use the iPad. In addition to showing you how to use Guided Access and Restrictions, this chapter also focuses on tips for helping educators and parents manage the apps on their iPads. One of the most powerful features of the iPad for people with disabilities is its support for third-party apps that can meet a wide range of needs. However, it can sometimes be difficult to find the right app to meet a certain need from among the wide selection available on the App Store. Likewise, as the number of apps installed on our iPads grows over time, it also becomes more difficult to know which apps we have installed and where to locate them when we need them. In this chapter, I share a few resources for finding and evaluating apps for students who have special needs, as well as tips for organizing your apps so that you can make more efficient use of your iPads with your students.

Universal Design for Learning (UDL) Guidelines

- *Multiple Means of Engagement:* One of the components of this guideline is creating a safe learning space. Using Guided Access, the educator or parent can help students stay on task by limiting distractions because students are not able to exit the current app to surf the Web or watch videos on YouTube when they should be doing their academic work. Similarly, the Restrictions feature can be used to prevent learners from accessing content that is inappropriate for their age or developmental level. Reducing threats and distractions to learning with the features discussed in this chapter can help students more effectively concentrate on the learning process rather than on competing demands for their attention.

Guided Access

Checkpoint 7.3—Minimize threats and distractions.

Guided Access was introduced in iOS 6 to address the concern some parents and educators had that students could become distracted from the learning task while using the iPad. With Guided Access, the parent or educator can launch an app and enable a single-app mode where the student is not able to exit the app by clicking the Home button. In the past, the only way to limit a student from exiting an app was to place a protective cover over the Home button, but with Guided Access, this is no longer necessary.

To use the single-app mode available with Guided Access, do the following:

1. Go to Settings > General > Accessibility > Guided Access, and tap the On/Off switch to enable Guided Access.
2. Tap Set Passcode and enter a four-digit passcode you can remember. Without this passcode, students will not be able to end a Guided Access session or change its options, so it is important that you not place the code somewhere the student could find it or use a code that could be easily guessed.

Figure 9.1   Guided Access Screen in Settings to Set a Passcode for Guided Access

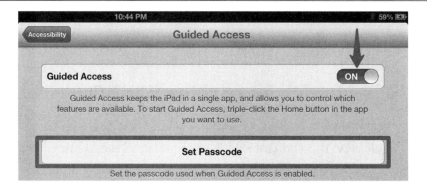

3. Once you have enabled Guided Access in Settings, launch the app you want to use in single-app mode.

4. Triple-click the Home button to start Guided Access. If you do not have any other accessibility features enabled for Triple-Click Home, you should see the Guided Access options. Otherwise, you may have to first select Guided Access from an Accessibility Options popover menu.

Figure 9.2   Accessibility Options Menu

5. At the bottom of the screen, you can choose to disable touch if you only want to use the iPad as a display or disable motion so that students are not able to change the orientation.

Figure 9.3   Buttons to Disable Touch and Motion in the Guided Access Options

6. Once you have selected your options, tap Start at the top of the screen. At that point, the only way a student can exit the app is by triple-clicking the Home button, entering the correct passcode, and choosing End.

Guided Access also has an option for disabling touch in certain parts of the current app. This option allows a teacher to decide which parts of the app students can use and which ones are off-limits. For example, the teacher can use Guided Access to limit access to an app's settings so students are not able to change the configuration of that app once it has been set to match their needs. For some apps that have many options, disabling access to the settings can save the educator or parent a lot of time that would otherwise be spent resetting or reconfiguring the app. To disable parts of the screen with Guided Access, do the following:

1. Launch the desired app and open the Guided Access options by triple-clicking Home.
2. Draw a circle around the areas of the screen you want to disable and Guided Access will try to guess which buttons or controls should be selected. You can refine the selection by moving the handles.

Figure 9.4   Selecting Area to Disable Buttons With Guided Access

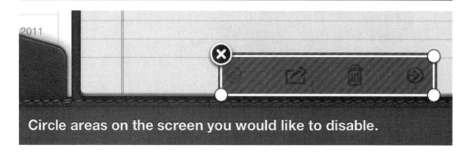

Circle areas on the screen you would like to disable.

3. Tap Start to begin the Guided Access session. While Guided Access is running, tapping on the areas of the screen that are disabled (grayed out) will not work.

QR Code 9.1
Guided
Feature of
Access iOS

To view a video tutorial demonstrating how to configure and use Guided Access, visit http://mobile learning4allbook.wordpress.com/2013/02/06/guided-access/ or scan QR Code 9.1.

Restrictions

Checkpoint 7.3—Minimize threats and distractions.

In addition to Guided Access, iOS includes a Restrictions feature that provides another option for parents and educators to exercise some control over the content students can access on their iPads. With Restrictions, parents and educators can block students from installing and removing apps, as well as use ratings to keep them from accessing music and other content that is not appropriate for their age or developmental level. Like Guided Access, Restrictions can be protected by setting a passcode that needs to be entered to disable the feature or make changes to how it is set up.

To use the restrictions feature, choose Settings > General > Restrictions, then choose Enable Restrictions. The first time you enable the restrictions, you will be asked to create and confirm a passcode to protect these settings. The Restrictions are organized into the following categories:

- Allow: Enable or disable individual apps such as Safari, iTunes, FaceTime, or the Camera. Other options prevent students from installing and removing apps, or from accessing the iBookstore. On devices that support Siri (third-generation or later iPad), you can also disable Siri, or limit the use of explicit language when using Siri. To change an individual restriction, tap the On/Off switch to the right of the app name or setting.
- Allowed Content: This includes options for controlling the type of content allowed on the device. After selecting the rating system for your country, you can limit students to accessing only movies, TV shows, and apps that meet a certain rating. You can also prevent students from accessing music and podcasts with explicit lyrics or books that have sexual content in them. An important setting in this section blocks in-app purchases. This is important because many free apps include an option for purchasing additional content (levels for games, characters, etc.) that could result in unwanted credit card charges if you don't block in-app purchases.
- Privacy: The settings in this section determine how much of your information apps can access on your iPad. You can prevent apps from accessing the information stored in Contacts, Calendar, and Reminders, as well as your location information, your Camera Roll, and Facebook and Twitter accounts.
- Allow Changes: The options in this section prevent students from making changes to the accounts used to manage Mail, Calendars, and Contacts. You can also prevent them from using Find My Friends, a location-based app for finding your friends and family on a map. The last option in this section is for preventing students from changing the volume limit you can set in

Settings > Music > Volume Limit. The volume limit is a good way to protect the hearing of your students.

- Game Center: This section only includes two settings. The first prevents students from participating in multiplayer games, while the second one prevents them from adding friends in games that support that feature.

To learn more about the Restrictions feature, visit http://mobilelearning4allbook.wordpress.com/2012/08/11/restrictions-in-ios/ or scan QR Code 9.2.

QR Code 9.2
Restrictions
Feature of iOS

Finding and Evaluating Apps

One way to stay up to date on the latest apps for a particular need is by following some of the sites and communities that focus on a specific population. Some examples of these types of communities include the following:

- AppleVis is a community-powered Web site for users of Apple devices who are blind or have low vision. The site maintains an iOS App Hall of Fame showcasing some of the best apps for VoiceOver users as nominated by the site's registered members.
- iAutism is a site that reviews apps in a number of categories related to autism (communication, motor skills, language therapy, etc.). This site is available in a Spanish version as well.
- BridgingApps features the Insignio App Tool for searching apps for children with special needs, creating app lists, and sharing and rating the lists.

A few apps are also available that collect reviews and links to other apps:

- Autism Apps is a list of apps being used with and by people with autism, Down syndrome, and related disabilities. The app includes more than 30 categories and the descriptions link to reviews and video demonstrations of the apps in action when they are available.
- Visually Impaired Apps (ViA) is an aggregator that sorts apps for people with visual disabilities by category, price, and iTunes App Store ratings. ViA also provides users with a forum to

suggest and discuss apps they find useful, and it gives them the power to track new apps as they become available.

In addition to these resources dedicated to apps for people who have special needs, a couple of communities for general educators include apps that may be helpful for working with students who have special needs. These sites are also a good place for finding apps focusing on academic skills (math, vocabulary, etc.).

- I Education Apps Review is a community of educators, administrators, and app developers with more than 30 volunteer app reviewers who look at the overall educational value of educational apps for iOS devices.
- Appitic.com is a directory of more than 1,800 apps curated by Apple Distinguished Educators.

To view these resources for finding apps to match your students' needs in one place, visit http://pinterest.com/mlearning4all/finding-apps/.

Many apps have lite or free versions that will let you try out most of the features before you buy the more full-featured paid version. This is an excellent way to test out apps to make sure they are a good fit for a student's particular needs. Another way to make a virtual evaluation of the app is to look it up on YouTube to see if someone has created a video demonstration that shows the app's key features and how to use it.

A number of educators have developed rubrics to help with app selection, and Tony Vincent has compiled a nice list of these rubrics on his Learning in Hand blog at http://learninginhand.com/blog/ways-to-evaluate-educational-apps.html. One of these rubrics, by Jeannette Van Houten, ties the selection of the app to a specific IEP goal and considers factors such as alternative access (how the app works with switch devices and other access tools). Along with these rubrics, the SETT (Student, Environment, Tasks, and Tools) framework developed by Joy Zabala can help ensure that apps are well matched not only to a student's needs and abilities but also his or her environment and the task for which the app will be used. More information about this helpful framework can be found on the author's Web site at www.joyzabala.com.

Purchasing Apps and Books

The iOS App Store is the online store where educators can purchase and download apps for their iOS devices. The iBookstore performs a similar function for books. Even for free apps and books, the App Store and iBookstore require an Apple ID to be created. Purchased apps and books are tied to this account rather than to individual devices, meaning that you can delete an app on a device and it is not gone forever. To recover the app, you would simply log in with your Apple ID on that device (or on another device if you are switching) to redownload it.

An Apple ID is generally set up with a credit card number, but if you only plan to download free apps and content for your classroom, it is possible to set one up without a credit card:

1. Make sure you are not logged into an existing Apple ID by going to Settings > iTunes & App Stores and tapping on the Apple ID and choosing Sign Out. Once you are logged out of your existing Apple ID, you can set up a new ID without a credit card.
2. Go into the App Store and select a free app to install on your device.
3. Tap Free followed by Install.
4. From the popover menu, choose Create a New Apple ID.

Figure 9.5   Popover Menu to Create New Apple ID

5. Make sure your country is selected under Store, and then tap Next. If the correct country is not shown, tap the name you see, and then use the picker to choose your country and select Done when you're finished.
6. Once you have agreed to the iTunes Store Terms and Conditions, tap Agree, and enter the requested information (valid email address, birthday to verify age, etc.).
7. Tap Next and choose None as the payment option.
8. Continue to fill out the requested information and tap Done when you see the email verification screen. This will inform you that you will receive an email for verification.

9. Open the email and tap the attached link. The App Store will open automatically and prompt you to sign in with your new Apple ID. Once you have signed in, you should see a thank-you screen. This is your confirmation that the new Apple ID has been set up without a credit card number.

Another option for purchasing apps is the Volume Purchase Program (VPP). This is a special program Apple created to make it easier for educational institutions to purchase apps and books in volume and distribute them to individual students, teachers, administrators, and employees. Apps that participate in the VPP are offered at a discount, but they must be purchased in bundles of at least 20 copies. The way the program works is a follows:

1. A designated program facilitator purchases the apps (or books) in volume using a credit card or other method of payment from the institution.
2. The program facilitator receives a unique code for each app (or book) and distributes that code to the student, teacher, or other person who will be using the app.
3. The individual teacher or student then goes into the App Store and redeems the code (by tapping on the Redeem option at the bottom of the Purchased screen).

Many free apps have additional options that can be added as in-app purchases (for example, additional levels for educational games, or features such as the option to export content created within the app). This is also the way in which many lite or free versions of apps are upgraded to the full version. To prevent unwanted purchases by students, in-app purchases can be restricted with the Restrictions feature discussed earlier in this chapter.

Organizing Your Apps

Checkpoint 7.3—Minimize threats and distractions.

Organizing apps into folders can make them easier to find for you and your students. You should also remove any apps you are not using not only to save space for your students' work but also to reduce the clutter on your iPad that might distract students from a task. The apps are associated with your Apple ID. Thus, if you later find that you need any of the apps you have removed from your iPad, you can just sign into the App Store again and download those apps.

To organize your apps on your device, tap one of the app icons and hold for a few seconds. When all the icons and folders start to move, you can edit your apps as follows:

- To delete an app, tap the X in the upper-right corner of its icon and choose Delete.
- To move an app, drag it to a new position on the screen (other apps will move to make space for it). To move the app to a different screen, drag the app's icon to the edge of the screen and hold until the screen flips, and then drop the app's icon in the desired position on the screen.
- To create a new folder, drop an app's icon on top of an existing app, enter a name for the folder, and tap anywhere outside the folder. Once the folder has been created, you can continue to drop apps into it until you reach its capacity.
- To remove an app from a folder, tap the folder's icon to open it, and then drag the app's icon until the folder closes, and you can drop it in an empty area of the screen.

When you're done moving and managing your apps, click the Home button so that the icons stop moving. Your iPad will also have a few apps in a Dock at the bottom of the screen. The apps in the Dock will always remain visible, even when you switch screens. The steps for deleting and moving apps from the Dock are the same as for apps in any screen. The Dock should be where you place apps that you know you or your students will use frequently so they are always visible.

Using the VoiceOver screen reader, you can manage the apps on your iPad even if you are not able to see the icons on the screen.

- To move an app with VoiceOver, select the app, then double-tap and hold until you hear VoiceOver announce, "Moving," followed by the name of the app. As you move the app around the screen, VoiceOver will continue to announce where you are on the screen, including the row and column number and whether you are inside or outside a folder (or on the Dock).
- To delete an app, double-tap and hold to enter the edit mode usually indicated by dancing icons, then double-tap again to bring up a notification that will ask you if you really want to delete the selected app. Choose Delete to remove the app from your device. These same techniques will allow you to close misbehaving apps from the App Switcher. VoiceOver will indicate when an app is removed from the App Switcher with a

tone. When you're done managing your apps with VoiceOver, click the Home button to exit the edit mode.

You can also organize your apps with iTunes while you have your iPad connected to your computer with a USB cable:

1. Choose your iPad on the right side of the screen (next to the iTunes Store button).

Figure 9.6 Button for Managing an iPad in iTunes

2. Select Apps. You should see a list of your apps, along with a preview area where you can see how they are arranged into screens on your iPad.
3. Use the Sort menu to sort your apps by name, kind, category, date, or size. You can also show all apps or only apps that have been designed specifically for the iPad.
4. To install apps you have previously purchased, click the Install button to the right of the app's name. You can also remove an app that has been already installed on the iPad by clicking the Remove button. To save your changes, click Apply at the bottom of the screen to perform a sync.

Figure 9.7 List of Purchased Apps in iTunes

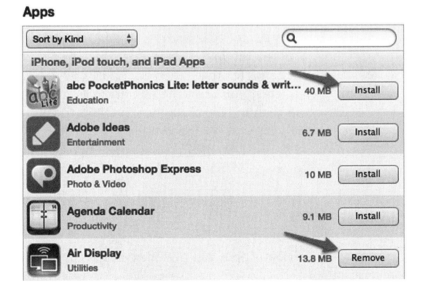

5. To move apps between screens, choose a screen thumbnail in the strip below the preview area, and then drag the app you want to move to a different screen than the one it is currently on. You can have up to 11 screens on your device.

Figure 9.8   Preview Area for Apps on an iPad Connected With iTunes

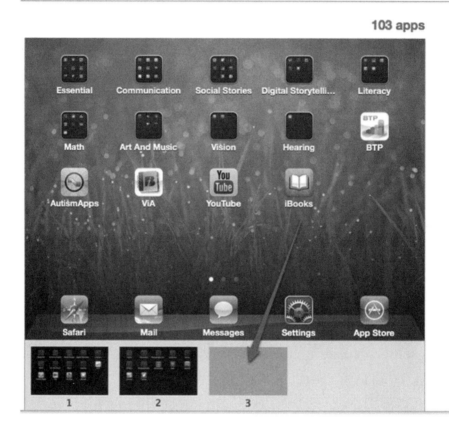

6. To organize apps into folders, drag an app on top of another app, until you see the folder instead of the target app's icon. Next, enter a name for the folder, and click anywhere on the preview area when you are done naming it. Once you have a folder, you can continue to drag apps into it until you reach its limit (currently 20 apps for the iPad).
7. When you're finished organizing your apps, choose Apply at the bottom of the screen to save your changes and sync your device.

iCloud

iCloud is a service from Apple that provides up to 5GB of free online storage. iCloud was developed to make it easier to transfer information and content between the many devices people now own. iCloud can be activated during the setup process for a new iPad (or one that has been updated to iOS 6) by entering a valid Apple ID and selecting Use iCloud. If you decide to skip the iCloud activation during your device's setup, you can still set up iCloud by going to the Settings, choosing iCloud, and entering a valid Apple ID. Once you have your Apple ID and iCloud configured, you can use iCloud to keep your calendar, contacts, email, reminders, notes, and Safari bookmarks synced across devices. To manage which items will be synced by iCloud, go to Settings > iCloud and tap the appropriate On/Off switches.

Figure 9.9   iCloud Sync Options in Settings

iCloud also has an automatic downloads feature that will keep apps, music, and books purchased through the Apple's online stores synced across devices. To use this feature, go to Settings > iTunes & App Stores and tap the appropriate on/off switch next to the desired items to sync (Music, Apps, or Books).

Figure 9.10   Automatic Downloads Options in Settings

Note that automatic downloads of purchased content (which includes free apps) can result in additional bandwidth use. If you are on a limited data plan, this can be an issue. I recommend turning off automatic downloads for the items you probably don't need to have on every device. For example, I probably don't want to read an e-book on the small screen of my iPhone or iPod touch, especially with my visual impairment. For e-books, I usually do not turn on automatic downloads, and I only download the e-books to the iPad, where I can read them on a larger screen.

The Photo Stream feature makes it easy to transfer photos between devices. Many of the communication apps allow you to create your own symbols with photos that represent the student's current environment. I recommend taking advantage of this option to make the communication more meaningful for the student. However, you may not always have the best camera on the device where you plan to use the communication app, or you may have the app installed on a device that does not even have a camera (like the first-generation iPad). With Photo Stream, you can take the photos with one device, and then transfer them to a different one. If you take a photo with your iPhone but you want to use it on the bigger screen of your iPad, all you have to do is open the Photos app on the iPad after you've taken the photo and the new photo will appear in the Photo Stream. The photos in your Photo Stream are only stored online for a month (30 days). To save them permanently, you have to save them to the Camera Roll or an album. This can be done as follows:

1. Open the Photos app on the device where you wish to save the photos.
2. Select Photo Stream at the top of the screen.
3. Tap Edit and select each photo you wish to save, then tap Share and choose Save to Camera Roll.

Figure 9.11   Sharing Options in Photos App

The Documents and Data option of iCloud can be helpful if a student has one device for use at school and another for use at home. With iCloud enabled on two devices with the same account, the student can begin working on a document on one device at school and finish it on a different device when she or he gets home. One thing to keep in mind about Documents and Data is that the documents shared with this option count against the iCloud storage limit of 5GB, unlike the other information that can be synced with this service. Another thing to keep in mind is that the transfer of large documents using this iCloud option can use a lot of the data on a limited service plan if you have a device that supports cellular data (such as one of the 3G/4G LTE versions of the iPad). If you are using iCloud-enabled apps (such as Pages, Keynote, or Numbers) and you are using a device with a cellular connection that has a limited data plan, you should go to Settings > iCloud > Documents and Data and set the on/off switch for Use Cellular to off to conserve the data allocated to your service plan. This option will only be available if your device has a cellular connection (iPad with 3G or 4G LTE).

You can use iCloud to do a complete backup of your mobile device. This can save a lot of time if your iPad has a problem and has to be restored to its factory default settings. With iCloud, you can restore your documents (including Camera Roll photos), settings, and information once you have installed a fresh copy of iOS to resolve the problem. As with Documents and Data, the backups you create with iCloud count against the 5GB of storage you get from Apple with a free account. You can purchase additional storage by choosing Settings > iCloud > Storage and Backup > Buy More Storage. If you decide not to use iCloud for backup purposes, you can still backup your device by connecting it to your computer with a USB cable and using iTunes to perform the backup.

In addition to syncing content and performing backups, iCloud has a Find My iPhone/iPad feature that can help you locate your device if it is lost or stolen. With this feature, you can remotely lock and wipe the information on your device if it is lost, as well as visit a Web site where you can see its current location and even send a message to anyone who finds it. This feature has already saved me once from a lost iPad, and I recommend all new iPad owners have it turned on. To turn on Find My iPhone/iPad, go to Settings > iCloud and tap the on/off switch for Find My iPhone/iPad.

Presenting With the iPad

There are two ways you can present from an iPad: You can connect your iPad to a TV or projector using an adapter, or you can do your presentation wirelessly through an Apple TV or an app that supports AirPlay mirroring. The HDMI adapter (available in both 30-pin and Lightning versions for $39 and $49, respectively) has the advantage that your iPad can charge while you are connected to the TV or projector. However, your classroom may have an older projector that does not have an HDMI option. In that case, you can use the VGA adapter, which like the HDMI one is also available in 30-pin and Lightning versions (for $29 and $49, respectively). With any of these adapters, you will be limited in how much you can move around the room as you present because you will need to be close to the HDTV or projector connection. The adapters will also tend to fall out causing a pause in your presentation that could be distracting to learners.

If you would rather move around the room while doing your presentation, then you can use an Apple TV (a $99 device used to purchase movies and other content for your TV) to connect to the projector or HDTV wirelessly. With this approach, you also don't have to worry about the adapter falling out because the connection is wireless. With an iPad 2 or later, you can then mirror everything on your iPad's screen to the external display. The one caveat is that both your iPad and the Apple TV have to be on the same Wi-Fi network for this work, and the HDTV or projector has to have an HDMI connector. I recommend this approach whenever possible, as it can help with classroom management by allowing you to move around the room to check on your students' progress and keep them on task as they work.

To use an Apple TV to present from your iPad, do the following:

1. Connect the Apple TV to an HD TV or projector with an HDMI cable.
2. On your iPad, bring up the App Switcher by double-clicking the Home button and flick to the right on the multitasking bar at the bottom of the screen until you see the AirPlay icon (a circle with a TV).

Figure 9.12   AirPlay Button in the App Switcher

3. Tap the AirPlay icon and select your Apple TV, and then tap the switch next to Mirroring.

Figure 9.13   Enable Mirroring in the AirPlay Pane

4. Tap anywhere outside the AirPlay popover, and then dismiss the App Switcher by clicking the Home button to work on your iPad as you normally would and have your work mirrored.

To stop mirroring your iPad or iPhone, open the AirPlay menu and set the switch for Mirroring to off. The mirroring feature can be helpful for performing demonstrations on a larger screen for students who have a difficult time seeing on the device itself. You can also use mirroring to allow students with mobility difficulties to show their work from where they are sitting. If you do not have an Apple TV, the iPad screen can also be mirrored to a computer using two different applications: Reflector (www.reflectorapp.com) and Air Server (www .airserverapp.com). With both, you must first install a helper app on your Mac or Windows computer, and then use AirPlay to establish a connection from your iPad just as you would with the Apple TV (your computer running Reflector or Air Server will appear on the list of available AirPlay devices). Versions of Reflector and Air Server are available for Mac and Windows, and Reflector even allows you to record what you do on the screen (including your audio). Both apps also allow multiple connections. If you plan to use the iPad to teach using a centers approach, you can mirror up to four devices so that you can see at a glance where each group is with their activity as you walk around the room.

Practice Activities

1. Enable Guided Access in the Settings, and set a passcode.
2. Launch your favorite app and start Guided Access by triple-clicking the Home button.
3. Try to exit the app by pressing the Home button. What happened?
4. Triple-click Home, and enter the passcode to get to the Guided Access options.
5. Circle a few areas of the screen to disable touch for them. Tap Resume and try to tap the parts of the screen you just disabled. What happened?
6. End your Guided Access session by triple-clicking Home, entering your passcode, and tapping End. Exit the app by pressing the Home button.
7. Disable Installing Apps and Deleting Apps in the Restrictions for your device. Try to install a free app from the App Store. What happened? Now try to delete an existing app from your device. What happened? When you are done, go back to Settings and remove the restrictions for installing and removing apps.
8. Turn on the editing mode on your iPad (when the icons jiggle) and practice moving apps to different screens, creating folders, and moving apps in and out of folders. When you're done, exit edit mode.
9. Delete an app from your device, then go into the App Store and practice reinstalling the app from your purchase history.

10

Challenge Based Learning With the iPad

Challenge Based Learning (CBL) is a framework for teaching and learning that seeks to make education more relevant and meaningful to all students. With CBL, students are engaged in authentic projects that call on them to find solutions to real-world problems in their communities. The idea is that students will be more engaged and motivated when the content closely matches what they are passionate about and when they are allowed to use the tools they are already familiar with and enjoy for personal use outside of school (including cell phones, tablets, and laptops).

Universal Design for Learning (UDL) Guidelines

- *Multiple and Flexible Means of Representation:* With CBL, students are given choices for accessing information from a variety of sources. Rather than relying on only the textbook, students can use the Web to research information, locate videos and other relevant media, and contact experts who can help them with the solution that will address their challenge.
- *Multiple and Flexible Means of Action and Expression:* Students are given choices for how they implement, evaluate, and document

their solutions to CBL challenges. While one team might create a video that raises awareness about a pressing issue in their community, another may choose other means to get their message heard (posters, a presentation to school leaders, etc.).

- *Multiple and Flexible Means of Engagement:* CBL is also a reflective process, and students are encouraged to reflect on their learning in a variety of ways throughout the process (through video reflections, blog entries, etc.). The goal of making students self-directed, reflective learners is also a key goal of UDL (Guidelines 7 through 9).

What Is CBL?

CBL is not a new idea. Its key concepts can be found in the work of John Dewey dating back to the 1930s (Johnson, Smith, Smythe, & Varon, 2009). Over the years, the real-world focus to teaching and learning behind CBL has gone by a number of other names, including project-based learning and problem-based learning. Both project-based learning and problem-based learning are instructional strategies that are intended to engage students in authentic, real-world tasks to enhance learning. Students are given open-ended projects or problems with more than one approach or answer intended to simulate the professional situations they will encounter in the world of work. Both learning approaches are also defined as student-centered and include the teacher in the role of facilitator or coach (guide on the side) rather than dispenser of knowledge (sage on the stage). Students engaged in project- or problem-based learning generally work in cooperative groups for extended periods, and they are encouraged to seek multiple sources of information. Often these approaches include an emphasis on authentic, performance-based assessment.

Despite these many similarities, project-based and problem-based learning are not identical approaches. Problem-based approaches structure students' activities more by asking them to solve specific problems rather than relying on students to come up with problems in the course of completing a project (Donnelly and Fitzmaurice, n.d.). However, as Donnelly and Fitzmaurice (n.d.) point out, it is likely that in practice the lines between the two approaches become blurred, and teachers use the two either in conjunction or as complements to each other. CBL builds on a similar tradition and extends much of the work that has been done on problem-based and project-based learning. However, at the center of challenge-based learning is a call to action that inherently requires students to not just learn about a topic, but also to make something happen in relation to that knowledge (Johnson et al., 2009). Students are compelled to research a topic and consider possible solutions because those solutions will improve their communities and have an impact on their lives.

Evidence for the effectiveness of these student-centered approaches is starting to build in the scholarly literature. A three-year 1997 study of two British secondary schools—one that used open-ended projects and one that used more traditional, direct instruction—found differences in understanding and standardized achievement data in mathematics. Students at the project-based school did better than those at the more traditional school both on math problems requiring analytical or conceptual thought and on those requiring rote learning. Three times as many students at the project-based school received the top grade achievable on the national examination in math (Edutopia, 2011). Similarly, a five-year study by researchers at SRI International found that technology-using students in Challenge 2000 Multimedia Project classrooms outperformed nontechnology-using students in communication skills, teamwork, and problem solving (Edutopia, 2011).

Regarding CBL, the most significant research to date was the pilot study the New Media Consortium and Apple conducted in 2008. In the fall of 2008, in six schools across the country with one-to-one laptop initiatives in place, both teachers and students found CBL effective and engaging, with 97% of the 321 students finding the experience worthwhile, and four out of five saying they would recommend the approach to other students (Johnson et al., 2009). Teachers unequivocally also rated the experience as positive, with every one of the 29 pilot faculty reporting that the work of the students exceeded their expectations (Johnson et al, 2009). A follow-up study that will explore whether the findings of the pilot study can be replicated beyond the high school focus of the first study was launched in January 2011, with the participation of 19 schools and universities. By visiting http://www.challengebasedlearning.org/pages/about-cbl, you can access more information about these research efforts related to CBL.

A Sample UDL Project

Checkpoint 7.1—Optimize individual choice and autonomy.
Checkpoint 7.2—Optimize relevance, value, and authenticity.
Checkpoint 8.3—Foster collaboration and communication.
Checkpoint 9.3—Develop self-assessment and reflection.

The CBL process begins with a big idea or issue that is important to students. Past CBL projects have focused on topics such as sustainability, violence, and apathy. From this big idea, students develop an essential question that places the big idea in the context of their community. The process continues with the articulation of a challenge that asks students to create a specific answer or solution to the challenge they have identified. To meet the challenge, students brainstorm guiding questions representing the knowledge they will need to gain to implement a workable solution, and they then participate in guiding activities to help them answer those questions. At the conclusion of the process, students document their solutions in a multimedia format that can be presented to the rest of the community. By focusing on an implemented solution, CBL makes it possible for students to be agents for change in their schools and communities.

With CBL, students with disabilities can work alongside their nondisabled peers to develop solutions to problems that impact their lives. What follows is one example of a CBL project focusing on identity and the meaning of disability. Throughout this project, students use their iPads and other mobile devices to reflect on the process and to document their solutions to the challenge. Mobile devices are a good fit for CBL because the framework requires students to work in their communities rather than be tied to their computers back in a classroom or computer lab.

Now that we have looked briefly at what CBL is, let us take a look at what this approach to learning looks like in practice through an example project that aims to provide a more inclusive community for all students.

Big Idea

Inclusion

Essential Question

How do I feel about ability/disability?

The Challenge

Promote empathy for the experiences of students with disabilities among their nondisabled peers and build bridges between the two groups by working together to address accessibility barriers in their school/community.

Guiding Questions

Who am I?

What do I do well?

What are my challenges?

How am I different from my classmates? How am I the same?

What does it mean to have a disability?

What are my beliefs about people with/without disabilities?

What can I do to make our school a more inclusive community for people of all abilities?

Guiding Activities

To meet their challenge, students can do the following:

- Use apps such as MindMeister and ThoughtsHD to brainstorm about their identity. Students start with their name in the middle and brainstorm things they are interested in and passionate about around it. Students then share these mind maps with one another in class and look for things they have in common.
- Use the Camera and Pages apps to create a photo essay of a typical day in their lives. Students will take images with the Camera app and use Pages to layout the images into a story that captures their daily experiences. The goal of this activity is to make students more aware of the challenges they face in their daily lives, as well as their daily victories and accomplishments.
- Use the Camera app or any video/audio recording app to interview someone in their community who has a disability (this could be a fellow student). Students then use the Camera app to record a reflection in which they address what they have learned from the interviews and how it has affected them personally.
- Use the Web browser on their iPads to research different disabilities on the Web.
- Use their iPads to document the accessibility of their learning environment, including the school buildings and facilities, the school Web site, and school communications. For example, students can make short videos documenting the difficulties a student with a disability would face accessing specific areas of their school buildings.

- Use their iPads to evaluate the usability and accessibility of their school's Web site on the mobile devices many of them own.

Guiding Resources

- iLearnToo wiki (http://www.ilearntoo.wikispaces.com)
- Part of Me, Not All of Me video: (http://www.youtube.com/watch?feature=endscreen&NR=1&v=sk-EtXk5iEg)
- About UDL from Center for Applied Special Technology Web site (http://www.cast.org/udl)
- Introduction to Web Accessibility from WebAIM Web site (http://www.webaim.org)
- Tech Ease 4 All Web site (http://etc.usf.edu/techease/4all/)
- Mobile Learning 4 Special Needs wiki (http://www.mbl4sn.com)

Solutions

A CBL project can have many solutions. In this example, one possible solution is that students use the knowledge they have gained through the guiding activities to identify the top-three accessibility challenges at their school (access barriers in the school Web site or issues related to access in the school's buildings and other facilities) and create a presentation to school leaders to make them aware of the issues they have identified.

Evaluation, Documentation, and Reflection

During the evaluation phase, students gauge the success of their solution through a variety of methods. For example, in the scenario discussed previously, students could use VoiceOver on their iPads to conduct a simple Web accessibility test on the school Web site after some time had elapsed to see if the problems they identified had been addressed, and then determine next steps (start a petition to be presented to the Webmaster, etc.). Throughout the entire process, the students could maintain a blog to document weekly progress on their project, any obstacles they'd encountered, and their steps to overcome these obstacles. Popular blogging platforms such as Wordpress or Tumblr have apps that make it easy to add posts from an iPad. The idea behind this step is to encourage students to reflect on the process as much as on the new content they have learned. As part of their documentation, students could use the cameras and apps on their iPads to create a short video about their solution and submit it to the

CBL community, where they could not only get feedback from others but also inspire others interested in implementing a similar project in their own community.

This chapter is only meant as a brief introduction to Challenge Based Learning. The Challenge Based Learning Community at www .challengebasedlearning.org has a more extensive description of CBL and many more example challenges to inspire you.

Conclusion

As you can see from the many accessibility features and apps I have discussed in each chapter of this book, we have come a long way when it comes to accessibility on mobile devices such as the iPad. Not only does iOS provide many built-in supports for vision, hearing, and motor skills, but through the many apps available on the App Store creative solutions have also been developed for students with learning, communication, and social difficulties.

I consider myself a good example of what accessible technologies can do for someone with a disability. Despite having a significant visual disability, I have been able to accomplish a number of goals I set for myself, including succeful completion of my doctorate. Without the many accessibility features Apple has created for people like me, I don't know that I would have been able to successfully pursue such a difficult goal. These technologies have played an important role in empowering me to accomplish my academic goals, and they have also enriched my life and brought me great joy by allowing me to pursue my passion to be an iPhoneographer (a photographer who uses an iPhone or an iPad for photography). I have written this book to help other educators provide the same opportunities for the students with disabilities in their classrooms. It is my hope that the step-by-step tutorials and other resources available through the QR codes provide you with the tools you need to implement Universal Design for Learning (UDL) and accessibility with iPads.

However, even as the accessibility of Apple's mobile devices continues to improve, an important challenge remains: the accessibility of the content available for these devices. By designing content in a way that follows a few simple accessibility best practices, content such as electronic books can be designed in a way that allows the accessibility features of the iPad and other mobile devices to work as intended. Where appropriate, I have included some techniques for designing accessible content in this book. For example, the chapter on visual supports included a section on how to include accessibility descriptions for images so that the VoiceOver screen reader can describe those images to people with visual disabilities, and in the chapter on auditory supports, I discussed captioning as a way to provide access for those with hearing disabilities. It is my hope that in addition to exploring new accessibility features and apps as they become available, you will also consider keeping your design skills up to date with the latest accessibility techniques to make sure there is synergy between your mobile device's capabilities and your ability to design accessible content. Both aspects of universal design are crucial to ensuring students of all abilities have the access to the curriculum to which they are entitled. I hope you will join me in promoting the next wave of accessibility for mobile devices, when the accessibility features of those devices and the content educators create for them work in concert to make sure all learners have equitable access to the curriculum.

Appendix A
Additional Resources

Apple Accessibility

http://www.apple.com/accessibility/
This is Apple's official page for product accessibility information and news.

AppleVis

http://applevis.com
This site includes app reviews and tutorials created by users who are blind or who have low vision. The app reviews often include information about VoiceOver compatibility.

MacVisionaries

http://groups.google.com/group/macvisionaries/about
This is a Google Group for Mac users with visual disabilities, including owners of mobile devices.

Eric Sailers.com

http://www.ericsailers.com/
This blog is by Eric Sailers, a speech language pathologist who frequently shares tips and resources for the use of mobile devices with students who have special needs.

Teaching Learners With Multiple Special Needs

http://teachinglearnerswithmultipleneeds.blogspot.com/
This excellent blog is by Kate Ahern, an experienced educator who works with students with multiple disabilities.

Teaching all Learners

http://teachingall.blogspot.com/
This is a blog by Patrick Black, a special education teacher from Mt. Prospect, IL.

AT Tips

http://www.attips.posterous.com
This is a blog by Cathy Hoesterey focusing on "clean and simple technology tips for all."

inov8's There's a Special App for That

http://www.inov8-ed.com/category/special-app-for-that/
Each post in this series from inov8 features a group of apps that address a specific need, from communication to literacy instruction and independent living skills.

iPhone/iPad Apps for AAC From Spectronics

http://www.spectronicsinoz.com/iphoneipad-apps-for-aac
This is a comprehensive and thorough list of apps for augmentative and alternative communication (AAC).

Mobile Learning 4 Special Needs

http://mobilelearning4specialneeds.wikispaces.com
This is a Wiki where I post many of the accessibility tutorials you can access through the QR codes in this book, as well as information about new apps and accessories.

Appendix B

VoiceOver Gestures

Basic Navigation

- Flick right or left to select the next or previous item.
- Double-tap anywhere on the screen to activate the selected item (such as open an app).
- Two-finger "scrub" (move two fingers back and forth three times quickly, as if making a "z") to go back to the previous screen, dismiss an alert, or close a folder.
- Three-finger flick left or right to go to next or previous screen.
- Three-finger flick up or down to scroll down or up one screen.
- Three-finger tap to provide additional information (such as the current page or screen, or the position within a list).
- Three-finger flick down while any item in the status bar is selected to open the Notification Center. Use the two-finger scrub gesture to dismiss the Notification Center.
- Four-finger tap to select the first/last item on the screen (this will depend on whether you tap on the top or bottom part of the screen).
- Double-tap and hold for one second to use a standard gesture. For example, you can double-tap and hold on a slider, then without lifting your finger drag to change the values controlled by the slider. Standard gestures are also helpful for moving apps or folders.
- Select the page indicator (the dots located between the Dock and the apps on the Home screen) and flick up to go to the next screen or down to go to the previous screen.

Note: Any time VoiceOver announces that an item is adjustable, as with the page indicator, you can change the value of that item by flicking up or down with one finger while the item is selected.

Device Functions

In addition to the gestures you use for basic navigation of the touch-screen interface, a number of VoiceOver gestures control device functions:

- Select the Unlock button and double-tap the screen with one finger to unlock your device.
- Two-finger double-tap will answer or end a call on the iPhone; play and pause in the Music, Videos, YouTube, and Voice Memo apps; take a photo in the Camera app; start or pause a recording in the Voice Memos and Camera apps; and start and stop the stopwatch.
- Three-finger double-tap to mute/unmute VoiceOver.
- Three-finger triple-tap to turn the screen curtain on and off. If you still hear VoiceOver but don't see anything on the screen, the screen curtain has been turned on.
- Triple-click the Home button to toggle VoiceOver off and on (this feature can be set up to toggle other accessibility settings such as Zoom and White on Black in the Settings app).
- Tap any letter on the onscreen keyboard and perform the scrub gesture (iPad only) to split or merge the keyboard.

iPad Multi-Touch Gestures

On the iPad, VoiceOver can be used along with the four- and five-finger gestures introduced in iOS 5:

- Four-finger flick left or right to switch apps.
- Four-finger flick up from the bottom of the screen to open the app switcher. Flicking down with four fingers will close the app switcher.
- Five-finger pinch to close the current app.

Appendix C

Keyboard Shortcuts for Using VoiceOver With an Apple Wireless Keyboard

VO Key Shortcuts

VO stands for VoiceOver keys (holding down the Control and Option keys on the keyboard at the same time).

- VO and Left/Right Arrow key: Navigate the items on the screen by moving the Voiceover cursor to the previous or next item, which can be an app or a folder (including ones in the Dock).
- VO + Space Bar: Select the current item (same as double-tapping).
- VO + "-": Same as double-tap (for answering calls, starting playback or recording).
- VO + H: Same as pressing the Home button. Using this shortcut from the Home Screen will take you to the Spotlight search screen. Pressing this shortcut twice in a row will bring up the app switcher to let you switch apps.
- VO + M: Move the focus to the status bar at the top of the screen.
- VO + S: Toggle the speech on/off.
- VO + Shift + S: Toggle the screen curtain on/off.
- VO + A: Read from the current item.
- VO + B: Read from the top of the current page or screen.
- Control by itself: Pause VoiceOver.
- VO + Command + Left/Right Arrow key: Cycle through VoiceOver speech settings (Volume, Speech Rate, Typing Echo, Use Phonetics, and Use Pitch).

- VO + Command + Up/Down Arrow key: Select a different value for the currently selected VoiceOver speech setting.
- VO + K: Turn on the VoiceOver help.
- VO + I: Open the Item Chooser.
- Escape key by itself: Go back, cancel, or dismiss popup (same as the scrub gesture).
- Command + Tab: Switch to next app (on iPad). Adding the Shift key will move switch to the previous app.
- VO + F: Open the search. Type your search term and press Enter to search for the first match.
- VO+ G: Move to the next search match. Add shift to move back to the previous search match.

In addition to the VO keys, the QuickNav feature available on the Mac is also supported:

- Left and Right Arrow keys at the same time: Activate/deactivate the QuickNav feature.
- Right or Left Arrow key: Move to the next or previous item.
- Up and Down Arrow keys at the same time: Select an item when QuickNav is turned on (this is the same as pressing VO-Space Bar).
- Option and one of the arrow keys: Scroll to another screen.
- Up and Right/Left Arrow keys: Turn the rotor clockwise or counterclockwise.
- Up Arrow or Down Arrow key: Select the next or previous option for the currently selected rotor setting.
- Control and the Up Arrow or Down Arrow key: Select the first or last item on the screen.

Safari Single-Key Shortcuts

- H: Next heading
- 1 to 6: Next heading of that level (heading level 1, heading level 2, etc.)
- L: Next link
- S: Next text element
- T: Next table
- X: Next list
- I: Next image
- B: Next button
- C: Next form element

References

Apple, Inc. (2012, January 19). Apple reinvents textbooks with iBooks 2 for iPad [Press release]. Retrieved from http://www.apple.com/pr/library/2012/01/19Apple-Reinvents-Textbooks-with-iBooks-2-for-iPad.html

Bonnington, C. (2012, January 20). iPad a solid education tool, study reports. *Wired.com.* Retrieved from http://www.wired.com/gadgetlab/2012/01/ipad-educational-aid-study/

Boyd, A. W. (2011, September 11). Adapting to the iPad, called education's 'equalizer.' *USA Today.* Retrieved from http://www.usatoday.com/news/health/wellness/special-needs/story/2011–09–11/Adapting-to-the-iPad-called-educations-equalizer/50362426/1

Center for Applied Special Technology (CAST). (n.d.). What is Universal Design for Learning? Retrieved from http://www.cast.org/udl/

Center for Applied Special Technology (CAST). (2011). *Universal design for learning guidelines version 2.0.* Wakefield, MA: Author.

Center for Universal Design. (2010). Ronald L. Mace. Retrieved from http://www.ncsu.edu/project/design-projects/udi/center-for-universal-design/ron-mace/

Disseldorp, B., & Chambers, D. (July, 2002). *Selecting the right environment for students in a changing teaching environment: A case study.* Paper presented at the meeting of the Australian Society for Educational Technology International, Melbourne, Australia.

Donnelly, R., & Fitzmaurice, M. (n.d.). Collaborative project-based learning and problem-based learning in higher education: A consideration of tutor and student roles in learner-focused strategies. *AISHE Readings.* Retrieved from http://www.aishe.org/readings/2005–1/donnelly-fitzmaurice-Collaborative-Project-based-Learning.html

Edutopia (2011). PBL research summary: Studies validate project-based learning. Retrieved from http://www.edutopia.org/project-based-learning-research

Hecker, Burns, Elkind, Elkind, & Katz. (2002). Benefits of assistive reading software for students with attention disorders. *Annals of Dyslexia, 52,* 244–272.

Johnson, L.F., Smith, R. S., Smythe, J. T., & Varon, R. K. (2009). *Challenge-based learning: An approach for our time.* Austin, TX: The New Media Consortium.

Leong, C. K. (1995). Effects of on-line reading and simultaneous DECtalk auding in helping below-average and poor readers comprehend and summarize text. *Learning Disability Quarterly, 18,* 101–116.

Montali, J., & Lewandowski, L. (1996). Bimodal reading: Benefits of a talking computer for average and less skilled readers. *Journal of Learning Disabilities, 29,* 271–279.

Riconscente, M. (2011). Mobile learning game improves 5th graders' fractions knowledge and attitudes. Los Angeles, CA: *GameDesk Institute.* Retrieved from http://www.gamedesk.org/reports/MM_FINAL_REPORT.pdf

U.S. Department of Education. (2010, June 29). Joint "Dear college" letter: Electronic book readers. Retrieved from http://www2.ed.gov/about/offices/list/ocr/letters/colleague-20100629.html

Wehmeyer, M. L. (2002). *Self-determination and the education of students with disabilities* (Digest No. E632). Reston, VA: ERIC Clearinghouse on Disabilities and Gifted Education. (ERIC Document Reproduction Service No. ED470036)

Wise, B.W., & Olson, R.K. (1994). Computer speech and the remediation of reading and spelling problems. *Journal of Special Education Technology, 12,* 207–220.

Index

CORWIN

A SAGE Company

The Corwin logo—a raven striding across an open book—represents the union of courage and learning. Corwin is committed to improving education for all learners by publishing books and other professional development resources for those serving the field of PreK–12 education. By providing practical, hands-on materials, Corwin continues to carry out the promise of its motto: **"Helping Educators Do Their Work Better."**